VIRAL
HATE

VIRAL HATE

CONTAINING ITS SPREAD
ON THE INTERNET

ABRAHAM H. FOXMAN
AND CHRISTOPHER WOLF

palgrave
macmillan

VIRAL HATE
Copyright © Abraham H. Foxman and Christopher Wolf, 2013.
All rights reserved.

First published in 2013 by PALGRAVE MACMILLAN® in the U.S.—a division
of St. Martin's Press LLC, 175 Fifth Avenue, New York, NY 10010.

Where this book is distributed in the UK, Europe and the rest of the world, this
is by Palgrave Macmillan, a division of Macmillan Publishers Limited, registered
in England, company number 785998, of Houndmills, Basingstoke, Hampshire
RG21 6XS.

Palgrave Macmillan is the global academic imprint of the above companies and
has companies and representatives throughout the world.

Palgrave® and Macmillan® are registered trademarks in the United States, the
United Kingdom, Europe and other countries.

ISBN: 978-0-230-34217-0

Library of Congress Cataloging-In-Publication Data
Foxman, Abraham H.
   Viral hate : containing its spread on the Internet / Abraham H. Foxman and
Christopher Wolf.
      pages   cm
   Includes bibliographical references.
   ISBN 978–0–230–34217–0 (alk. paper)
   1. Hate crimes—Prevention. 2. Online hate speech. 3. Internet—Moral and
ethical aspects. 4. Hate speech. I. Wolf, Christopher. II. Title.
   HV6773.5.F69   2013
   364.15—dc23
                                                                    2012047877

A catalogue record of the book is available from the British Library.

Design by Letra Libre

First edition: June 2013

10 9 8 7 6 5 4 3 2 1

Printed in the United States of America.

*To my wife, Golda; and our children, Michelle and Ariel;
son-in-law, Dan; and my grandchildren, Leila, Gideon,
and Amirit for their love and encouragement; and to all
who support ADL's efforts to fight bigotry, stereotypes, and
anti-Semitism.*

—Abraham H. Foxman

*To my husband, Jim, for his support and encouragement;
to my extended ADL family—professional staff, lay leaders
and supporters—for recognizing the importance of Internet
hate as an issue for society to address; and to the Internet
community for its willingness to tackle the difficult issues
raised by hate speech.*

—Christopher Wolf

CONTENTS

ACKNOWLEDGMENTS

ABRAHAM H. FOXMAN:

This book has been many years in the making, and it deals with a subject that both Chris and I have wanted to address in long form for some time. Yet if we had completed this project several years ago, it would have been a very different book. With technology changing so rapidly, we are facing a much different and much more complex set of circumstances today than we were even just three or four years ago.

From the earliest years of the Internet era it became clear that the haters would be among the first to not only recognize the incredible potential of this technology, but successfully exploit it for their own ends.

The haters and the bigots were among the first to create web sites devoted to racist and anti-Semitic messages. And it was the Internet—this incredible tool for social interaction, information sharing, and commerce—that brought the distribution of prejudice and bigotry into the twenty-first century. As hate spread virally, the Internet, out of force of necessity, became a major new focus of our work at the Anti-Defamation League.

Over the years, Chris and I have each in our own way contributed to the fight to stem this rising tide of electronic hate.

Chris, in his professional life, became a well-known expert in the field, and over the years he volunteered much of his free time representing ADL on this issue before a variety of important international forums, as well as to corporations and governments. I am deeply grateful to him for his service in this arena. He has always been there to share with us his knowledge of the issues and the law. His enthusiasm is infectious and his expertise unrivaled.

Several others have helped along the way as Chris and I worked to take this project from concept to reality.

I am especially indebted to Karl Weber for his ongoing partnership, his patience, and his ability to listen and help me translate my thoughts and ideas into this book. He is my literary partner and a special friend.

I say thank you to my agent, Lynne Rabinoff, who, as always, lent her support, enthusiasm, and dedication to the project.

I am grateful to the Anti-Defamation League's current national chair, Barry Curtiss-Lusher, and past chair, Robert G. Sugarman, for their support and faith in this project and in me.

A special thank you goes to several of my ADL colleagues who provided welcome guidance and support throughout this undertaking: Ken Jacobson, for his wise counsel and insight; Deborah Lauter and Steve Freeman for their advice and acumen; Steve Sheinberg for his thoughtful recommendations; and Myrna Shinbaum and Todd Gutnick for their tireless efforts in helping to keep this project on track and see it through to its completion.

CHRISTOPHER WOLF:

It is my great privilege to be a lay leader of the Anti-Defamation League, and to be able to marry my professional focus on Internet law with the mission of the ADL "to stop the defamation of the Jewish people and to promote justice and fair treatment for all." I am deeply grateful to my coauthor, Abe Foxman, ADL's national director, for involving me since 1995 in the League's work to address Internet hate and, of course, for asking me to coauthor this book with him.

Abe is an inspirational leader. I am one of the lucky ones he has inspired over the years. I know of no other person as passionate about standing up for what is right, as committed to fighting hate, or as dedicated to a cause.

Abe's prodigious communications skills are well-known. But Abe would be the first to admit he is not an "early adopter" of communications technology. Still, he recognizes how the Internet gives unprecedented power to anti-Semites and bigots of all kinds to spread their messages of hate. Abe had the vision early on to make Internet hate an agency priority, and as a result, ADL is recognized as a leader on the subject, as it is on so many civil rights issues. In representing the League in international bodies and at global conferences, it is gratifying indeed for me to see the respect given to ADL and its work.

Abe's ADL legacy will be multifaceted, and fighting online hate will be an important part of that legacy.

This book serves as an emblem of Abe's and the ADL's important work. This book and ADL's substantive efforts on Internet hate would not have been possible without the dedication of ADL professionals, including Ken Jacobson, Deborah Lauter, David Friedman, Steve Sheinberg, Steve Freeman, Robert Trestan, Jonathan Vick, and many others. It is an honor for me to work with these professionals, as I now do in my capacity as National Civil Rights Chair for the ADL. I thank my friend and ADL National Chair Barry Curtiss-Lusher, as well as his predecessors, for the opportunities to serve in leadership roles at the ADL, which led to my opportunity to coauthor this book with Abe.

My personal thanks go to Karl Weber for his indispensable and collaborative role in creating the book, and for his patience. And thanks to agent Lynne Rabinoff for helping get the book from concept to publication, and to Palgrave Macmillan for recognizing the importance of the subject we are addressing.

Thanks, too, to my law partners at Hogan Lovells US LLP for their commitment to pro bono and civil rights, and for allowing me the time to work on this book and all of my ADL projects. Donating the royalties from this book to the ADL is another small way the firm and I are expressing our support of the League's important work.

Finally, my thanks and love to my spouse, James L. Beller, Jr., a playwright, whose faith in me and insights throughout the creation of this book made all the difference.

INTRODUCTION

I n November 2012, this book's two authors were in Chicago for a meeting of the Anti-Defamation League's (ADL's) National Commission on the occasion of the kick-off to ADL's one hundredth anniversary year. Unhappily, the meeting coincided with the dramatic escalation of attacks from the Gaza Strip on Israel and Israel's military response. Throughout the Chicago sessions, ADL leaders were monitoring the situation on their iPhones, iPads, and BlackBerries, looking for YouTube videos, tweets on Twitter, and Facebook postings linking to the latest news. Newspapers, radio, and television news played a minimal role in keeping us abreast of the latest events; instead, we turned instinctively to the Internet and the burgeoning array of social media as the most up-to-the-minute sources of information.

We couldn't help recalling a similar event seventeen years earlier, on November 4, 1995. On that date, the authors were also in Chicago, participating in another ADL National Commission meeting. It was the day when Israeli Prime Minister Itzhak Rabin was assassinated. Our meeting obviously was interrupted by the first reports of the tragic and terrible shooting. TV news was sketchy, so we turned to the then-novel tool of the Internet to try to learn more. Accessing the home page of the *Jerusalem Post* website took a long time, and then all we saw was the static contents of the morning's print newspaper with only a one-line text bulletin about the shooting.

How times have changed—and how quickly. Today whenever there is urgent news, millions of people around the world turn first to the Internet, where abundant news sources instantly and thoroughly inform us.

In 1995, one of the reasons we were meeting was that we realized even then that hate groups were using the Internet as a powerful and growing tool to spread their evil messages of intolerance and rage. For one hundred years, ADL has been fighting anti-Semitism and hate of all kinds. So when hate went online, we knew we had to address it. As early as 1985, ADL published a report entitled *Bulletin Boards of Hate,* addressing what today seems like a quaint method of online communication—dial-up bulletin boards. In 1995, the first official ADL task force to focus on online hate was formed, and it continues its vastly expanded work today, relying on knowledgeable and committed ADL professionals and guided by volunteer lay leaders.

With each advance in Internet technology, from the appearance of websites and the interactivity of AOL through the blossoming of social media sites like Facebook, Twitter, and YouTube and the recent explosion in mobile computing, we have seen how anti-Semites, racists, anti-Islamists, homophobes, misogynists, anti-immigrants, and other kinds of haters have embraced the new technologies to spread their lies, to recruit, and to mislead. Almost as bad is the bad behavior by otherwise good people who use the comment sections of online news stories and services like Facebook and YouTube to vent their hidden hatreds or generate dark humor at the expense of minorities.

We frequently refer to the spread of hate online as a "virus" whose infection spreads much as a disease spreads through a vulnerable population. We're reminded of the beginnings of the AIDS epidemic in the 1980s, when knowledge of the virus was scarce but awareness of its horrible effects was slowly growing. The virus of hate online does not kill directly, but, as we describe in this book, its effects can be lethal. Online hate is a serious illness that normalizes bigotry, diminishes discourse, misleads kids, and blights the lives of its online targets. This phenomenon has been too slowly recognized.

For both of us, fighting hate—online and off—is an essential part of our lives. One of us is a Holocaust survivor whose entire professional career has been with the ADL, serving since 1986 as national director. The other is a practicing Internet/privacy lawyer and longtime ADL lay leader who has made pro bono civil rights work an essential part of his career. We each have experienced and witnessed, in different ways, anti-Semitism, homophobia, and other forms of hate. We have joined together to write this book to share our combined professional knowledge of the issue of Internet hate, to raise awareness of the seriousness of a rapidly growing societal problem, and to propose ways in which good people—including the leaders of the Internet industry—can address the problem without compromising our vital historic commitment to freedom of expression.

The old schoolyard chant "Sticks and stones may break my bones, but words can never hurt me" is no longer true, if it ever was. Words of hate hurt—they can even kill. But there is no reason that society needs to stand by, silent, while people suffer. There's a better way. That is why we wrote this book.

Abraham H. Foxman and Christopher Wolf
November 2012

HATE DOESN'T JUST HURT—IT KILLS

I n February 2009, the U.S. Holocaust Memorial Museum in Washington, D.C., mounted an unusual exhibit. Building on the museum's mandate to document and memorialize the murder of six million Jews, its exhibit entitled *State of Deception* focused on the power of Nazi propaganda. It traced Hitler's program of extermination back to its roots in the manipulation of German mass media and popular culture. The exhibit showed how the Nazi propaganda machine used the media of the day—movies, posters, newspapers, magazines, books, pamphlets, and paintings—to skillfully spread lies about Jews and to reignite and perpetuate centuries-old anti-Semitic stereotypes. It also showed how the Nazis crafted racist messages that were more nuanced and subtle than one commonly recalls—messages that were designed to persuade and ultimately desensitize the general population, not just fanatical followers. Thus, *State of Deception* showed how Nazi propaganda helped create a nationwide climate of hatred, suspicion, and indifference that ultimately laid the groundwork for Hitler's "final solution."

One Nazi-sponsored painting in the exhibit effectively showed the power of deceitful and incendiary words. Depicting a youthful Hitler giving a speech before a handful of captivated followers, the painting was titled, *In the Beginning Was the Word*—an apt description of the almost magical power of words—of propaganda—to produce unimaginable evil.

The evil of the Nazi regime was vanquished almost seventy years ago. But the power of words and images to propagate hate remains a force of evil in our world. Today, there are powerful new tools for spreading lies, fomenting hatred, and encouraging violence. Ironically, they are the same tools that have enriched society by creating new ways to communicate, educate, and entertain. They are the tools of the Internet.

In a little more than twenty years, the Internet has blossomed as a way to connect the world. But, at the same time, the openness and wide availability of the Internet that we celebrate has sadly allowed it to become a powerful and virulent platform not just for anti-Semitism but for many forms of hatred that are directly linked to growing online incivility, to the marginalization and targeting of minorities, to the spread of falsehoods that threaten to mislead a generation of young people, to political polarization, and to real-world violence.

Hitler and the Nazis could never have dreamed of such an engine of hate. Online anti-Semites are joined by Islamophobes, racists, misogynists, homophobes, and other kinds of vicious haters. Turn over a single rock in this netherworld of the Internet and you may be amazed at the number and variety of repellent attitudes and threats that suddenly become visible. The most virulent hatemongers are joined by a growing number of normally right-minded people who employ the shield of online anonymity to say horrible, hurtful, and hateful things in comment sections and elsewhere across the Internet, adding to the deterioration of civil discourse.

Of course, the new technology of propaganda exhibits some dramatic differences from the old. Instead of being under the central control of a political party or group, the power of the Internet lies in its viral nature. Everyone can be a publisher, even the most vicious anti-Semite, racist, bigot, homophobe, sexist, or purveyor of hatred. The ease and rapidity with which websites, social media pages, video and audio downloads, and instant messages can be created and disseminated online make Internet propaganda almost impossible to track, control, and combat. Links, viral emails, and "re-tweets" enable lies to self-propagate with appalling speed. Hate begets hate, and its widespread appearance makes it seem increasingly acceptable and normal in a world where traditional standards of honesty, tolerance, and civility are rapidly deteriorating.

A few years back, we might have dismissed the anti-Semitic groups, racist organizations, and other vicious haters on the Internet as outliers—fringe elements relegated to obscure websites, not worth taking seriously or responding to. But today we live in the world of Web 2.0, which has transformed the way the Internet is being used. In the interactive community environment of Web 2.0, social networking connects hundreds of millions of people around the globe; it takes just one "friend of a friend" to infect a circle of hundreds or thousands of individuals with weird, hateful lies that may go unchallenged, twisting minds in unpredictable ways. And with the users of Web 2.0 comprised largely of younger people, the impact of the misinformation contained there may persist for generations to come.

In the years since the advent of YouTube, Wikipedia, Facebook, MySpace, Twitter, and other Web 2.0 technologies, we have seen a sudden and rapidly increasing wave of bigotry-spewing videos, hate-oriented affinity groups, racist online commentary, and images encouraging violence against the helpless and minorities—blacks, Asians, Latinos, gays, women, Muslims, Jews—across the Internet and around the world. Undoubtedly as new technologies continue to evolve, new ways to communicate and connect online will be developed—and as these innovations emerge, new tactics for the promulgation of hatred will also appear.

HOW HATRED PROLIFERATES ON THE INTERNET

The ways in which the Internet is being used to disseminate and promote hateful and violent beliefs and attitudes are astounding, varied, and continually multiplying.

Websites Promoting Extremist Groups

Every extremist organization has its website—often more than one. Such websites are sources of hateful propaganda, lies, and incitements to violence that would otherwise be relegated to the shadows.

Organizations dedicated to promoting tolerance and freedom, including ADL, the Southern Poverty Law Center, the Simon Wiesenthal Center, and others, have made it part of their mandate to keep tabs on the ever-changing landscape of extremist politics in the United States and around the world. There are dozens of groups, large and small, many with overlapping memberships, parallel agendas, and sometimes shared leadership rosters. From time to time, these groups fold, merge, splinter, or rename themselves, meaning that tracking their current configurations can be quite a challenge. They include neo-Nazi organizations, offshoots of the Ku Klux Klan and other racially centered movements, rabidly anti-government militia groups (which often identify themselves using code terms such as "survivalist," "constitutionalist," and "sovereign," among others), quasi-religious groups that cloak their racist and ultra-conservative agendas in rhetoric about "Christian identity" or "religious freedom," and many other variations.

Some of the most notable organizations in this rogues' gallery of hatemongers include:

- Stormfront, one of the earliest extremist websites with a sizeable Internet presence, claiming an active membership well over 250,000. Founded by Don Black, a Klan veteran who spent three years in prison for participating in an armed attempt to seize power in the Caribbean island of Dominica, Stormfront maintains an Internet forum with over nine million posts, an online radio program, a site that hosts user-generated blogs, and a large library of propaganda resources. Some of those who visit the

site and participate in its myriad opportunities for online sharing, chatting, blogging, and organizing do more than just talk
about their beliefs. Some apply them to violent actions in the real
world. In a 2009 shooting, Richard Poplawski, a poster on the
site, was charged with ambushing and killing three Pittsburgh
police officers and attempting to kill nine others.

• Hammerskin Nation, the most violent and best-organized neo-
Nazi skinhead group in the United States. Launched in Texas in
the late 1980s, Hammerskin Nation has spread to include skinhead groups in locations around the United States, focused mainly
on recruiting disaffected young people through music and racist
propaganda. A number of its members have been convicted of
harassing, beating, or murdering minorities. Many popular racist rock bands are affiliated with Hammerskin Nation, and the
group regularly sponsors concerts. The well-designed Hammerskin Nation website, coordinated by the Eastern Hammerskins
in New Jersey, features concert reviews, chapter listings, and local
contacts.

• The National Socialist Movement (NSM), currently the largest
neo-Nazi group in the United States, with members in forty-
seven states. With roots dating back to the 1970s, NSM is currently led by Jeff Schoep, who has made an effort to link the
movement to separate skinhead and Klan organizations. The
NSM promotes its virulently anti-Semitic and racist ideology
at rallies throughout the country. Between 2009 and 2011, the
group's rallies focused mainly on anti-immigration rhetoric. The
group promotes its message through its website, a white power
music company, and violent, propagandistic video games.

• The New Black Panther Party for Self Defense (NBPP), the largest organized anti-Semitic and racist black militant group in
America. The group is led by Malik Zulu Shabazz, a Washington,

D.C.–based attorney who has been active with the NBPP since the mid-1990s. By taking on racially charged issues under the guise of championing civil rights, the NBPP has received national media attention for its efforts, garnered some support from prominent members of the African American community, and attracted followers. However, although the NBPP's website and other outlets make an effort to appear mainstream (for example, with a message offering President Obama "Congradulations [sic]" on his re-election victory), the vast majority of African American and civil rights groups and leaders have rejected its racist orientation and its calls for revolution against "the hells of Amerikkka."[1]

The role of the Internet in propagating violence extends beyond the way it provides fodder for the distorted worldviews of individual fanatics. It also allows anti-Semites, racists, and bigots to communicate, collaborate, and plot in ways simply not possible in the offline world. Online recruiting has allowed many hate groups to increase their membership. In fact, Don Black, former grand dragon of the Ku Klux Klan, noted that, "as far as recruiting, [the Internet has] been the biggest breakthrough I've seen in the 30 years I've been involved in [white nationalism]."[2]

Some hate-oriented websites go so far as to target specific individuals. One familiar example is the infamous Nuremberg Files site, created by anti-abortion activist Neal Horsley, which publicized the names, addresses, and family data of physicians who provided abortion services in a thinly veiled effort to invite physical attacks on these doctors. (We'll discuss this case in more detail in a later chapter.) Another example, less well known, is that of Bonnie Jouhari, a fair housing advocate from Reading, PA, who also happens to be the mother of a biracial child (Jouhari herself is white). Apparently these qualities aroused the ire of extremist Ryan Wilson, leader of a Philadelphia neo-Nazi group called Alpha HQ, which made Jouhari the target of an extraordinary hate campaign:

> In March of 1998, a white supremacist Web site in the United States began posting pictures of Jouhari's workplace exploding amid animated .gif flames. The Web site featuring Jouhari was modified a few months later to include hate speech attacking Jouhari's child, describing her as a "mongrel." Soon after, a car began regularly following Jouhari home, she received harassing phone calls at work and at home, and she has moved several times to get away from this ongoing threat to her life and the life of her child.[3]

In 2000, a court ordered Wilson to pay damages of $1.1 million to Jouhari, but this victory was largely hollow, since the defendant had few assets from which payment could be drawn. In a separate case the same year, Roy E. Frankhouser, a self-described "Ku Klux Klan chaplain," was found guilty of participating in Jouhari's harassment and ordered to perform community service as restitution. However, these victories in court didn't end Jouhari's nightmare. She and her daughter fled across the country to Seattle, but the threatening phone calls and harassment followed them. As of late 2008, they were searching for yet another home, wondering whether they would ever find sanctuary from the real-world consequences of online hate.[4]

Cloaked Websites

Thanks to search technologies that are subject to shrewd manipulation, a fringe group's bigoted website can end up being ranked among the leading search results for a given topic on Google and other search engines, thereby achieving the kind of worldwide viewership once reserved for authoritative, mainstream messages. Many extremist groups have taken advantage of this characteristic of the Internet to create what are often called "cloaked websites"—pages that masquerade as impartial sources of factual information about social, historical, or political topics but are actually founts of hate-filled propaganda. The goal is to lure students and other curious would-be researchers into reading and believing content that would almost never find its way onto the shelves of a reputable school, college, or public library.

Cloaked websites are often cleverly constructed to mask both their origins and purposes. They are given URLs (web addresses) that sound neutral, such as www.martinlutherking.org and www.AmericanCivil RightsReview.com (the latter currently inactive). Some, such as the website of the Institute for Historical Review (IHR.org), are sponsored by pseudo-academic groups whose names may sound impressive to the uninitiated but whose work has been repeatedly exposed by serious scholars as shoddy and inaccurate.

The sites' home pages look innocuous; for example, the American Civil Rights Review site had a home page featuring a picture of Malcolm X and the slogan, "Speaking Out For The New Civil Rights Movement." This benign facade was designed to lull students, parents, and teachers into assuming that the site was a legitimate one, perhaps created by a civil rights organization. Only once the visitor began clicking on links that lead deeper into the site was the real nature of the content revealed. In the case of the Review site, the "inner" pages of the site included articles that purported to demonstrate that African American slaves were treated well and actually benefited from slavery, links to information about former Ku Klux Klan leader David Duke's political campaigns, stories about the "racism" of Jesse Jackson, and even an article supposedly showing that the famous African American scientist George Washington Carver did *not* invent peanut butter. (Undoubtedly there were some actual "facts" scattered through these and the many other weird contents of the Review site, but to present this melange as an unbiased overview of the American Civil Rights movement, as the site did, is beyond ludicrous.)

It's not surprising that the American Civil Rights Review site was so outrageously biased. It was created by Frank Weltner, a St. Louis–based member of the neo-Nazi National Alliance organization who also maintains the anti-Semitic website www.Jewwatch.com. Deception on the Internet seems to be part of Weltner's standard operating procedure; in the wake of Hurricane Katrina, he ran several phony sites that scammed people out of money they intended to donate to help the victims (a judge in St. Louis had to issue a restraining order against these sites).[5]

Social Media Pages

Facebook, YouTube, Twitter, Tumblr, Pinterest, and other social media sites are used by hundreds of millions of people around the world. The overwhelming majority are decent citizens who enrich the culture of the Internet with positive and often highly creative contributions; their reports of local, family, and civic activities; and their advocacy of charitable, artistic, or social causes. But some are rabid haters who use the largely uncensored, uncontrolled pages of social media sites to spew abuse, lies, propaganda, and vitriol against those they deem less worthy—and to encourage others to do the same.

One example of how haters are abusing social media websites occurred on the Fourth of July, 2010. As Americans were celebrating their nation's birthday, a new event was announced on Facebook—"Kill a Jew Day." The Facebook host for the event wrote, "You know the drill guys," and he urged followers to engage in violence "anywhere you see a Jew" between July 4 and July 22. A Nazi swastika adorned the official event page on Facebook. That posting prompted a wave of anti-Semitic rants on Facebook in support of the targeting of Jewish people. (Happily, as we'll discuss later, the story did not end there.)

Other hatemongers of various stripes have used the wide-open spaces of Facebook to post content promoting their favorite hobbyhorses, often using language and images that cross the line from "edgy" into offensive or even threatening:

- As the 2012 presidential election neared, Facebook pages loaded with racist mockery and attacks on President Obama and the first family proliferated. One page featured comments such as, "Obama needs to step down and go back to Africa with the rest of the coons!! He's nothing but a jigaboo and spear chucker!" Another included a Photoshopped image of the president wearing heavy gold jewelry and a baseball cap, gripping a bucket of fried chicken, and asking, "Where all the white wimmin at?"[6]

- Despite complaints from women's rights activists in the United States and Britain, pages dedicated to "jokes" about rape posted by male Facebook users continued to pop up across the social media. The supposed humor included such remarks as, "I love raping bitches out in the cool night air, don't complain sluts or your [sic] next," and "You know she's playing hard to get when your [sic] chasing her down an alley."[7]

- Numerous Facebook pages have been created that deny the Holocaust, praise the Nazis, and blame Jews for the "economic troubles" faced by Germany during the interwar period. One typical page is titled "Everyday Jokes on Holocaust Hoax"; another, titled, "Holocaust . . . History of Hoax," includes a video of a self-proclaimed scholar evaluating Hitler's policies and concluding that, despite "some racist points," he offered "an otherwise very beautiful program that was very successful, all in all."[8]

- Even Facebook pages created by legitimate businesses have been hijacked by bigots using newsworthy controversies as excuses to spread hate. When the Lowe's home improvement store chain decided to withdraw its ads from the TLC network show *All-American Muslim*, the Lowe's Facebook page (which ironically was festooned with joyful symbols of the Christmas season) erupted with vitriolic comments identifying Islam with terrorism. Typical examples: "At least with you Muslims here we know you won't be running down the middle of the street yelling 'Allah Akbar' and shooting or blowing anyone up!" and "ring ring Hallo? yes dis is Muslim flight school. . . . We teach you to fly but not how to land . . . free halal burger after each lesson too."[9]

Other social media sites have not been immune to invasions from the same kind of virus of hate: Twitter, Tumblr, YouTube, and all the others have been plagued with similar problems. As we'll discuss in a later chapter, the companies that manage these sites are aware of the issues and have made efforts to address them—but the plague of hate speech shows little sign of abating.

Games

"Online gaming" has a benign sound, and most Internet games are indeed harmless. But shrewd propagandists have learned how to use the popularity of computer gaming to insinuate racist and other hateful attitudes into the minds of young people. Consider, for example, the game *No Hope for Haiti*, posted on Stormfront.org, which challenges players to bomb survivors of the Haiti earthquake, or neo-Nazi–themed games with titles like *Aryan Test*, *Clean Germany*, *Anti-Turk Test*, and *KZ Manager* (which assigns players the task of running a concentration camp).

Even mainstream computer games, such as the war games in the popular *Call of Duty* series, played competitively on popular mainstream gaming sites like the XBox Live service provided by Microsoft, have been infected by hate speech. The violent nature of the games themselves, combined with the anonymity prevalent in online gaming sites, encourages players to indulge freely in fantasy behaviors that would be unacceptable in real life. These behaviors can include the use of hate speech—such as racist, ethnic, anti-Semitic, misogynistic, and homophobic slurs—against opponents. A journalist who recently investigated the problem ran across numerous examples of language and attitudes that the uninitiated would find hair-raising: "One gamer told an opponent [that] he presumed to be Jewish that he wished Hitler had succeeded in his mission. Many exchanges involve talk of rape or exult over the atomic bombing of Japan. There are frequent slurs on homosexuals, Asians, Hispanics and women."[10] Some gamers who are black, Jewish, gay, female, or members of other minorities that are subject to abuse have been driven from the pastime by this hostile, threatening atmosphere.

Merchandise Sales

Huge numbers of online sites sell hate-oriented books, games, records, movies, posters, Nazi memorabilia, and other products that very few reputable retailers would stock. Hidden from public scrutiny, shoppers easily find these distasteful goods on the Internet. Obvious examples are such "classics" of hate literature as Hitler's autobiographical *Mein Kampf*, the notorious Russian forgery *The Protocols of the Elders of Zion* (which purportedly details the secret age-old Jewish plot for global dominance), and the 1978 novel *The Turner Diaries* by William Pierce (which describes a genocidal race war to "liberate" the United States, ending in the killing of all Jews and racial minorities in the country). Timothy McVeigh, the Oklahoma City bomber, left behind a dog-eared copy of *The Turner Diaries,* and his terrorist attack in April 1995 closely mirrored a fictional bombing of FBI headquarters in that book.

Well-known works of bigotry like these are just a fraction of the weird, dangerous materials available online. Many others detail the "secret history" of sinister manipulation behind institutions ranging from the United Nations and the Federal Reserve to the Hollywood movie industry (and, of course, ADL). Other books offer practical advice for would-be terrorists and "resistance fighters," including lessons in creating and using explosives, rockets, kidnapping, and guerrilla warfare techniques. Every book sold, of course, produces revenue for the hate groups that sell it as well as introducing or reinforcing the virus of bigotry in impressionable minds.

An even greater money-maker for extremist groups may be music. So-called "white power" music, a politically charged amalgam of such familiar styles as punk rock, hard rock, and skinhead sounds, has been a recognized phenomenon since the 1980s, attracting interest and loyalty, especially among the disaffected young people who are prime targets of hate group recruitment.

Most white power music is now distributed by a handful of companies with significant online presences. The pioneer in the field is Resistance Records, founded in 1993 and based in Michigan. It sold as many as 50,000 CDs a year before experiencing legal troubles that eventually led to its purchase by the late William Pierce. Pierce, then the leader of the National Alliance, at the time the largest neo-Nazi group in the United States, moved Resistance to his West Virginia headquarters. He saw that Resistance not only could be a lucrative source of funds, but could also spread the influence of the National Alliance in the white supremacist world. He gave the company to Ohio National Alliance leader Erich Gliebe to run.

The main competitor to Resistance—and for many years the leader in white power music sales—was the Minneapolis-based Panzerfaust Records. Started in 1998 by Anthony Pierpont and former Resistance employee Eric Davidson, the company had strong ties to racist skinheads in the United States, especially to Hammerskin Nation, the largest racist skinhead group, which organized concerts that Panzerfaust sponsored.

One reason for Panzerfaust's relative success has been its ability to link hate music with the white supremacist cause. In September 2004, for example, Panzerfaust announced "Project Schoolyard USA," an explicit attempt to recruit children by using hate music. Panzerfaust created a special compilation CD of hate music that it sold for just pennies, intending for white supremacist groups to buy large numbers of the CD and distribute them to children at schools, concerts, and other venues. A number of white supremacist groups enthusiastically endorsed the scheme.

In addition to Panzerfaust (now Tightrope) and Resistance, smaller racist music labels and distributors abound in the United States, including Diehard Records (Chesapeake, OH), Micetrap Records & Distribution/RAC Records (Maple Shade, NJ), MSR Productions (Wheat Ridge, CO), White Power Records (Wilmington, NC), and Final Stand Records (Newark, DE). Racist music distributors can be found around the rest of the world, too, from the H8 Store in Germany to Ash Tree Records in Italy. However, the U.S.-based distributors play a very important role in shipping white power music around the world—even to those countries that may prohibit it, such as Germany.

International Hatemongering

The power of the Internet to facilitate instantaneous global communication makes it a powerful tool for those who seek to expose injustice and spread democracy. But it is also a powerful tool for those whose goal is to inflame tensions among groups in conflict. Combined with other modern communications technologies (broadcast television and radio, cable and satellite distribution, cellular telephony), the web brings far-flung groups in contact with one another, creating unprecedented opportunities for inter-group friction, hatred, and violence. As Susan Benesch, director of the World Policy Institute's Dangerous Speech project, has written:

> People are increasingly privy to communication that they would not have heard (or read or seen) in the past, namely the internal language of other, disparate cultural communities—the songs that members of a group sing together, the jokes they tell to one another, and the words their leaders use to rally supporters, to teach fear and hatred of others outside the group, or to inspire violence.
>
> Muslims from Afghanistan to Saudi Arabia learn that the prophet Mohammed has been lampooned (and to them, defiled) by cartoonists at a provincial Danish newspaper, feminists discover Facebook pages where men gather to trade rape jokes among themselves, and rural Afrikaners hear of a Zulu song that they fear may be catalyzing violence against them in the racially charged atmosphere of present-day South Africa.[11]

Many of today's most artful hatemongers take shrewd advantage of the global reach of the Internet as well as the maze of varying international laws and regulations regarding online hate speech. (We'll discuss the challenge presented by differing national rules in detail in a later chapter.)

The story of Gary Lauck offers an illustrative example. Based in Lincoln, NE, Lauck has been nicknamed "The Farm Belt Fuehrer"—though American-born, he sports an affected German accent and a bristly Hitler-style moustache, proud emblems of his conversion to Nazism at the tender age of eleven. In 1974, Lauck founded the NSDAP/AO, the German-language acronym for National Socialist German Workers Party/Overseas Organization, which is officially dedicated to promoting "a worldwide National Socialist-led White Revolution for the restoration of White Power in all White nations."

For years, Lauck risked arrest by engaging in propaganda activities in his self-appointed homeland of Germany. He smuggled illegal caches of millions of anti-Semitic neo-Nazi items—books, magazines, newspapers, pamphlets, posters, films, computer disks—into Germany and helped "underground" leaders launch neo-Nazi cells in several German cities. Finally, in 1995, Lauck was arrested in Denmark on an international warrant. (Simultaneously, German authorities raided the homes of around eighty Lauck followers—many of them teenagers—and seized weapons and ammunition along with piles of propaganda.) Lauck was extradited to Germany and sentenced to four years in prison.

Upon his release in 1999, Lauck discovered that the world of neo-Nazi recruitment had changed dramatically. The game-changer was the Internet. It was no longer necessary for would-be fuehrers like Lauck to take personal risks in transporting hate screeds across borders; now the World Wide Web could beam such messages into any computer at the click of a mouse. In 2001, back home in Nebraska, Lauck established his own web-hosting company, Zensurfrei.com ("censor-free" in German), which seeks out European clients in search of technological safe havens for hatred. Lauck's website declares, "Political repression is increasing in Europe! European webmasters can reduce their risk by moving their website to the USA!"[12]

Other web-hosting companies followed Lauck's lead. Sites like odinsrage.com and first-amendment-hosting.com catered to foreign individuals and organizations that want to use the relatively shielded environment of the United States as a home base to bombard European countries with hate-promoting content. (They also served American hate groups; for example, first-amendment-hosting.com provided the Internet connection for the website godhatesfags.com, produced by the Westboro Baptist Church, the Topeka-based group that became infamous for its homophobic pickets at military funerals.[13])

It's ironic: The same technology that connects the world and thereby can help teach people to understand and respect one another can also be used by those who want to foment intolerance and violence, spreading hatred across international borders.

~

This, then, is just a sampling of some of the many forms that viral hate has taken on the Internet. Perhaps most alarming is the way online hate has a way of morphing, spreading, and multiplying. Many practitioners of viral hatemongering aren't content with one or two targets or just a single way of disseminating their wares. Instead, they create virtual empires that spew vitriol at a wide range of objects and use numerous tools to connect with—and warp—the minds of those who stumble upon them.

Consider, for example, the British "political activist" Simon Sheppard. His U.S.-based website does business under the name of Heretical Press, which makes it sound like a publisher of offbeat materials espousing minority views on various topics. But if you spend a few minutes scrolling through the contents, you'll be amazed at the number and variety of enemies Sheppard imagines have infiltrated Western society. Sheppard hates Jews, of course, and does a good business in selling screeds that deny the Holocaust and mock Jewish victims—for example, a comic book titled *Tales of the Holohoax* that includes pages labeled "Alice in Lampshade Land," "Auschwitz: The Holiday Camp for Kikes," and "Kike Windchimes." (Some fan of Sheppard's pushed a copy of the book through the door of the Blackpool Reform Synagogue, apparently just for the thrill of offending and horrifying its members.)

But Sheppard also publishes pamphlets that rail against blacks, gays, and women (especially feminists) and denounce a wide range of nine-teenth- and twentieth-century thinkers, from Darwin and Pavlov to Freud. And Sheppard's website also distributes materials on such obses-sions as cannibalism and his weird theories of sex alongside seemingly harmless excerpts from the works of mainstream writers like Doug-las Adams (*Hitchhiker's Guide to the Universe*), Isaac Asimov, and H. L. Mencken. (The latter may serve as "starter drugs" that attract innocent web surfers to Sheppard's site, where the other materials then lure a certain percentage into less savory pursuits.)

In 2009, Sheppard and his partner Stephen Whittle were found guilty under British law of eleven counts of "publishing racially inflam-matory material." They fled to America, seeking asylum under U.S. laws that generally protect the free speech of even vicious hatemongers. (We'll delve more deeply into the varying treatment of hate speech un-der laws in different countries in a later chapter.) But U.S. Immigration and Customs Enforcement denied them asylum, and they were forced to serve brief prison terms in Britain. Today Sheppard is free, though legally banned from accessing the Internet.[14] Throughout the trial, Sheppard and Whittle were staunchly supported by the British People's Party, a neo-Nazi group. This is another sign of how viral hate works: Individuals and groups who share these repulsive views create formal or informal ties to one another, providing "mirror websites" to preserve content that has been taken down, offering financial and moral sup-port, and making it even harder for authorities or well-meaning op-ponents to isolate and combat them.

Or consider, as another example, the myriad uses of the Internet practiced by Tom Metzger, a former Klan leader who founded his own hate group, WAR (an acronym for White Aryan Resistance). Metzger's main website, www.resist.com, offers access to his newsletter, *WAR;* his cable access television show, *Race and Reason;* his radio program; a

merchandise page selling Aryan-branded t-shirts, caps, and other para-
phernalia; and a selection of violently racist, misogynistic, and homophobic video games.[15] In a world where digital media offer numerous
interactive ways of connecting with people of varying tastes, interests,
and communication styles, savvy hatemongers like Metzger are learning how to employ them all, in the process multiplying their ability to
affect—and infect—a broad swathe of humanity.

FROM WORDS TO DEEDS:
THE REAL-WORLD IMPACT OF ONLINE HATE

We can all agree that online sites and activities like the ones we've been
describing are vicious and disgusting. But does the dissemination of
hatred on the Internet really spawn violent behavior by individuals?
Maybe the best way to answer that question is through some real-life
examples.

Consider the story of James von Brunn, the eighty-eight-year-old
man who was charged with first-degree murder for the 2009 shooting of a security guard at the same Holocaust Museum where the *State
of Deception* exhibit appeared. Before the advent of the Internet, von
Brunn was a self-proclaimed white supremacist, an anti-Semite, and a
Holocaust denier—a garden-variety hater of a kind that, sad to say, has
existed for centuries. But in the old days, he would have been relegated
to using mail to communicate his rage to like-minded individuals, and
the only place for him to have his benighted views applauded might be
in a secret meeting hall down a dark alley somewhere.

The Internet changed all that. Like so many bigots, von Brunn
soon discovered that instantaneous electronic communication could
be a boon to his warped causes. He maintained a website called Holy
Western Empire, where he touted and provided excerpts from his self-
published book denying the Holocaust and lauding Hitler. And through

the use of chat rooms, online bulletin boards, and links to other haters' websites, von Brunn created a virtual online fan club that cheered on his vicious thinking.

Of course, we'll never know whether his rage would have burned out but for the Internet. But we do know that von Brunn found validation in the rage that he harbored on the Internet because it allowed him to interact, easily and continuously, with like-minded people who otherwise might be very difficult to find. Rather than being forced to deal with the real world, hate-filled paranoiacs can live in a universe of violent fantasies twenty-four hours a day thanks to the miracle of the Internet. (Von Brunn died of natural causes in January 2010 while in prison awaiting trial.)

Von Brunn was far from unique. In a 2009 case that shocked the city of Brockton, MA, a twenty-two-year-old woman was raped, shot, and wounded in her home by an assailant who also shot and killed her sister and, a few minutes later, a homeless man on a nearby street. What did the three victims have in common? All were black people who happened to be recent immigrants from the West African country of Cape Verde. Their alleged attacker was Keith Luke, a white loner who showed up in court with a swastika carved into his forehead. (As of this writing, Luke is awaiting trial for his apparent crimes.)

Luke told police he was "fighting for a dying race" and "fighting extinction" on behalf of the world's white people, racial views that he apparently developed through six months of continual visits to racist websites like Podblanc, which celebrates racial attacks and "lone wolf" domestic terrorism. A police report noted, "Luke told us that people on these sites spoke the truth about the demise of the white race."[16]

The influence of online hate propaganda is apparent in the background of other violent crimes. Benjamin Nathaniel Smith, an Indiana University student, went on a shooting rampage in July 1999, in which he killed two people and wounded nine others, all members of various racial or ethnic minorities. Smith was a devoted follower of Matthew Hale, founder of the World Church of the Creator, a white supremacist group famous for its use of the Internet to recruit members, especially children. Hale himself was later convicted of solicitation of murder and obstruction of justice, and sentenced to forty years in prison.[17]

Also in 1999, British neo-Nazi David Copeland planted nail bombs in a black neighborhood, a Bangladeshi area, and a gay pub in London, killing three and injuring more than a hundred. Copeland later proudly wrote, "I bombed the blacks, Paki's, [and] Degenerates," and he boasted, "I would of [sic] bombed the Jews as well if I got a chance." Copeland was sentenced to six life sentences for his crimes. Investigators discovered that he had learned how to build his bombs in a cyber-cafe, where he downloaded copies of *The Terrorist Handbook* and other manuals of destruction.[18]

Thus, the impact of online hatred is real and measurable. In the United States, incidents of cyber-bullying, violence against women and homosexuals, and bombings of abortion clinics all have been facilitated by the Internet and often have been inspired by content found on the Internet and encouraged by like-minded haters online. Neo-Nazis, skinheads, militia groups, and other extremist organizations have recruited vulnerable individuals online, some of whom have gone on to attempt acts of violence—sometimes with success. In Europe and South America, Jews have been threatened and beaten on the street and synagogues have been firebombed, often by individuals who drew inspiration from online sources.

Experts offer varying theories as to the nature of the link between online hate speech and real-world violence. Some emphasize the power of racist, anti-Semitic, homophobic, or otherwise bigoted websites to help focus and harness free-floating feelings of anger against specific targets. Sociologist Kathleen Blee describes the effect this way:

One thing we know from studying hate violence on the Internet and other media is that when people have violent or racist ideas, they are often very vague, very amorphous. What the Internet does is get people to focus, to make their racist and violent ideas much more coherent and much more targeted toward particular kinds of people. If you have somebody who is predisposed toward violence or predisposed toward racism, even vaguely, this can really gel [his or her] ideas. They [racist websites] give people a sense that violence is not only possible for somebody to commit, but laudatory.[19]

Other experts emphasize the role of the Internet in providing extremists with the feeling of empowerment that comes from believing that their feelings are widely shared. Psychologist Elizabeth Englander explains:

One of the things they're always looking for is validation, for evidence they're right, that their thinking is not crazy. Without the Internet, without global instant communication, you might have a few people in a community with a very extremist view, but there wouldn't be anybody else who shared their view. They might come to the conclusion that these extremist views are wrong or incorrect or kooky. With the Internet, they can always find others who share their views. Suddenly there is a community that says, "You're not crazy, you're right." That's very powerful.[20]

Social psychologist Phyllis Gerstenfeld adds, "The Internet creates the illusion of a larger community than really exists. You don't know if that chat room consists of one person or 1,000 people. [But i]t can help justify their beliefs or underscore their beliefs."[21]

Hate crimes do not represent a mere handful of isolated incidents. Thousands are reported every year, but experts agree the numbers are probably understated. Victims are often afraid to report what has happened to them; local authorities sometimes downplay hate crimes as "young people misbehaving" or "a crazy guy getting out of control." An exhaustive 2005 study by the Bureau of Justice Statistics suggested the number of hate crimes could be much higher than generally believed, a possibility that underscores the need to take this problem very seriously.[22]

The band Faithless got it right when it sang, "Racism is a weapon of mass destruction." Today the Internet provides a delivery system for that weapon more powerful than any the world has yet seen.

A POISONED CULTURE

What's more, hatred on the Internet has the power to impact not just a few fringe individuals but also the thinking of a wide swath of humanity. Internet hate speech serves to mislead millions of innocent people—especially young people who are enthusiastic users of new technology—thereby recruiting the next generation of bigots, racists, sexists, homophobes, and anti-Semites.

Blogging and social media sites are changing the way people communicate their reactions to events in the news and interact with each other. Those who harbor hate-based beliefs are comfortable expressing themselves in cyberspace, where they can provoke a reaction from others or find like-minded individuals to affirm their attitudes. That was the case following the news of the $50 billion Ponzi scheme engineered by financier Bernie Madoff. The blogs and online comments to news articles about Madoff were ablaze with anti-Semitic stereotypes attributing Madoff's crime to his Jewish background and using the incident as an excuse to blame "Jewish schemers" for the then-erupting global financial crisis.

Hate speech on the Internet is so pernicious because the more one sees it, the more one is likely to consider it normal and acceptable. Good people may sometimes become numbed by the sheer proliferation of vicious lies and daunted by the seemingly enormous task of responding. And others who are open to persuasion (due to youth, ignorance, or lack of sophistication) consider the worst of what they see as a reflection of what is acceptable in society. Whether consciously or not, they may think, "I see these ideas everywhere on the Internet—there must be *something* to them!" That's the real danger of online hate propaganda: It's like the Nazi propaganda of the 1930s and '40s, which was designed to lull the general population into tolerating steadily increasing doses of anti-Semitism.

With newspaper readership and television viewership in decline, people are getting their information elsewhere—online. And online is where today's virus of hatred is being spread. Countless websites portray gays and lesbians as subhuman under the guise of promoting "family values"; others spew racial epithets and caricatures; still others disseminate lies and phony rumors about politicians, religious groups, and organizations they oppose. In their wake, an online culture has developed—aided by the mask of anonymity—in which people who would never consider themselves members of hate groups employ racial, religious, and other epithets as part of their vocabulary in posting comments to news stories on mainstream websites and elsewhere online. In turn, the common appearance of such epithets desensitizes readers, making hate speech and the denigration of minorities appear "normal."

Many observers now feel that the uncontrolled flow of content on the Internet has helped fuel a steady decline in standards of civility governing how people interact with one another—sometimes with deadly results.

When Rutgers student Dharun Ravi set up a spycam to catch roommate Tyler Clementi in a same-sex romantic moment and then tweeted about it, he thought he was merely pulling a mean-spirited prank. Little did he know, his actions would drive Clementi to commit suicide. Ravi was subsequently sentenced to thirty days in prison and has become a national symbol of the dangers of cyber-bullying and homophobia. A few minutes of "online fun" and one person is dead, and another's life has been permanently tarnished.

So hate speech on the Internet is not just a theoretical problem. Nor is it merely a matter of civil discourse or of maintaining a higher standard of decency in our approach to matters of politics, religion, and social issues—important as that is. It can literally be a matter of life and death—the difference between a society where all of us feel safe walking down the street, knowing we will not be targeted for attack because of our race, religion, ethnicity, gender, or sexual orientation, and one where fear is a constant companion.

"All right," you may be saying. "I can see that online hatred is a serious matter. But can anything be done about it? Isn't the Internet like the old Wild West—a place where there are no rules, and where anyone is free to do and say anything?" That's an important and complicated question—one that we intend to answer in detail in the chapters that follow.

WHAT IS INTERNET HATE?

As we've seen, the familiar and comforting notion that "words can never hurt me," to quote from the old "sticks and stones" nursery rhyme, is sadly discredited in the Internet age. Words and images that appear online can easily be used to recruit and indoctrinate hatemongers and provoke violence. Hate speech can also mislead impressionable young people, perpetuating stereotypes and dangerous untruths. And for vulnerable minorities, hate speech can reinforce discrimination, with all of its disabling effects, and deter online participation by those attacked.

So we can all agree that hate speech on the Internet is a serious problem—but solving it, even conceptually, is far from easy. The challenge begins with the problem of defining Internet hate.

HATE SPEECH AND A MURDER IN LIBYA— LESSONS FROM *THE INNOCENCE OF MUSLIMS*

The Innocence of Muslims case offers a fascinating and troubling illustration of the complexities of the challenge of defining Internet hate. Does the term "hate speech" include any content that is gross, disrespectful, and insulting? Is content that many find offensive and that triggers (or is used as a justification for) violence safely classified as hate speech? Or is something more required before a particular form of expression is classified as hate speech, triggering a legal or societal response?

As most of the world now knows, *The Innocence of Muslims* is a crudely produced fourteen-minute movie trailer virulently critical of the religion of Islam and its founder, Muhammad, whom it depicts as a killer, womanizer, and child molester. The video does not expressly call for violence against anyone and does not fit into the category of hate speech as defined by most online services, including YouTube, where it appeared. Produced quickly in 2011, the video was made available on YouTube, but for months it attracted little attention. Then, early in September 2012, an Egyptian-American blogger publicized the video in an Arabic-language post and in an English-language email newsletter known for its celebration of the notorious Koran-burning Florida pastor Terry Jones. Jones had previously announced plans to stage an anti-Islamic demonstration on the anniversary of the September 11th terrorist attacks.

This confluence of inflammatory events helped make the video newsworthy. Riots and demonstrations denouncing the video took place in Egypt, Libya, Iran, and Yemen. In Benghazi, Libya, the protests heightened the tension and confusion surrounding a terrorist attack on the American consulate that took place at the same time and led to the death of Ambassador J. Christopher Stevens and three other Americans.

The protests and riots in response to *The Innocence of Muslims* put YouTube and its parent company, Google, in an awkward position. On the one hand, Google has always maintained that it strives to avoid removing user-generated content from the sites it controls. This "anti-censorship" stance is both a practical business decision (the more content available via social media sites like YouTube, the more visitors they are likely to attract) and an ethical position based on the historical American commitment to freedom of speech. In the words of company executive Rachel Whetstone, Google has a "bias in favor of free expression—not just because it's a key tenet of free societies, but also because more information generally means more choice, more power, more economic opportunity and more freedom for people."[1]

Yet what about a video that was believed, at first, to have played some role in four deaths—and that was used as a basis (or, some say, a pretext) for continuing violent protests that were spreading to other countries in the region, with the potential of triggering still more violence? Was Google's commitment to free speech strong enough to withstand these practical realities and the social and political pressures they generated?

The answer was no (at least outside the United States). By midday the day after the killings in Benghazi, YouTube decided to use its technological capabilities to pull *The Innocence of Muslims* from its servers in particular Muslim countries. The company released an email explaining its decision:

> We work hard to create a community everyone can enjoy and which also enables people to express different opinions. This can be a challenge because what's OK in one country can be offensive elsewhere. This video—which is widely available on the Web—is clearly within our guidelines and so will stay on YouTube. However, given the very difficult situation in Libya and Egypt we have temporarily restricted access in both countries. Our hearts are with the families of the people murdered in Tuesday's attack in Libya.[2]

Soon thereafter, Google announced it had also deleted *The Innocence of Muslims* from its servers in India and Indonesia, where the content of the film ran afoul of local laws against materials that attack religion.

In time, the demonstrations ceased, the furor died down, and the inflammatory film returned to the shadows of obscurity where it belonged. But the episode raised countless questions about Google's role as a global soapbox for all kinds of political views, the nature of freedom of speech in the Internet age, and the issue of how to balance community sensibilities against the importance of open expression. Critics faulted Google's action from several directions. Some pointed out that blocking the video in specific countries would be unlikely to prevent anyone who really wanted to see it from finding it elsewhere; others worried that pre-emptive "censorship" by Google seemed to "reward" those who chose to protest free speech with violence, giving them what's known as a "heckler's veto"; and still others wondered about how a for-profit company subject to all sorts of financial and political pressures could be expected to be a stalwart champion of freedom of speech while trying to do business in a global environment. As one journalist put it, "Google is acting like a court, deciding what content it keeps up and what it pulls—all without the sort of democratic accountability or transparency we have come to expect on questions of free expression and censorship. It has gone into uncharted waters, and it has taken us along with it."[3]

There's another element to this story that has been little noted but that makes it an even more disturbing example of how ethnic and religious bigotry can make reasoned, honest discourse all but impossible—particularly in an era when truth and falsehood can both be disseminated worldwide in the twinkling of an eye. According to some early news reports, a man who identified himself as the film-maker initially told some journalists that he was an "Israeli-American" named "Sam Bacile," and the film had been made possible by funds from a hundred Jewish donors. That information was apparently not corroborated before it was published, but it quickly spread through the news media, word of mouth, and the incalculable power of the Internet. *The Innocence of Muslims* became, in the minds of millions, an example of "Jewish Islamophobia" and a symbol of how two ancient religions were locked in a death struggle to control the Middle East using every means available—including the power of scurrilous propaganda.

It was an easy story to believe, one that fit neatly into the preconceptions of plenty of observers. But it was completely false.

In fact, we now know that *The Innocence of Muslims* was actually the handiwork of a Californian of Egyptian Coptic origin named Nakoula Basseley Nakoula, and that "Sam Bacile" is evidently a completely fictitious character. (In November 2012, Nakoula was ordered to return to prison by a California court for violating the terms of probation set when he was freed after a 2010 conviction for bank fraud.)

Although these facts have now been widely reported, the damage has been done; many who heard the initial reports may not have been exposed to the later corrections. It is still not clear why the purported film-maker claimed a Jewish identity, and whether he was motivated by anti-Semitism or merely intended to deflect the blame onto a convenient scapegoat group. Regardless of the motivation behind this lie, the story quickly spread through the social media. It led to a call from the Iranian leadership to protest the film as a piece of pernicious Jewish propaganda and undoubtedly has further fed the anti-Semitic fantasies of those already primed to believe in conspiracy theories. Yet another deplorable consequence of the sad confluence of forces—prejudice, resentment, hatred, and bigotry, all fueled by instantaneously electronic communication—that combined to make *The Innocence of Muslims* debacle possible.

∿

A reflexive reaction to all of this might be "There oughta be a law." What social purpose is served by allowing private citizens to inflame international tensions through the production and dissemination of a valueless, ahistorical video with the apparent goal of exacerbating religious hatred? Why not simply forbid such actions—through the power of law, if necessary?

The answer to this seemingly commonsense question is a complex one. As we'll discuss in greater detail later in this book, the First Amendment sharply—and, in our judgment, wisely—restricts the ability of the U.S. government to pass laws that unduly limit free speech.

Admittedly, U.S. law permits exceptions to be made in cases where speech is "directed to inciting or producing imminent lawless action." (In the famous words of Justice Oliver Wendell Holmes in the 1919 case *Schneck v. the United States,* "The most stringent protection of free speech would not protect a man falsely shouting fire in a theater and causing a panic.") Would *The Innocence of Muslims* video, possibly produced with at least the partial intent of inciting anger, and perhaps violence, among those whom it attacked, be eligible for legal restriction under this rule? We personally do not think so, despite the objectionable nature of the video. The fact is that it's impossible to craft a legal rule that clearly and consistently separates legitimate dissent from content created solely to incite others.

Yet opinions differ, even among experts. Journalist Anthony Lewis, a staunch defender of freedom of the press and author of a well-known history of the First Amendment, believed it might. "Based on my understanding of the events," Lewis said in an interview, "I think this meets the imminence standard. . . . If the result is violence, and that violence was intended, then it meets the standard."[4]

By contrast, Leslie Harris, president and CEO of the Center for Democracy and Technology and a respected authority on freedom of speech issues, has observed that *The Innocence of Muslims* may not even qualify as hate speech by the standards of most Americans. "I think they would consider it obnoxious, unpleasant, but both as a matter of law and of cultural norms, I think there would be a substantial number of Americans who would not view it as hate speech. . . . We have shows on Broadway like *The Book of Mormon* that pokes fun pretty directly at Mormons. We have *The Life of Brian,* making humor out of the story of Jesus. So for a variety of reasons, including the amateurish nature of *The Innocence of Muslims*, I find it hard to take it seriously as a threat to peace."[5]

It's clear that U.S. law could not have been used to prevent the dissemination of *The Innocence of Muslims* and the violence it may have helped to provoke. U.S. courts have been reluctant to overturn the presumption that freedom of speech is a fundamental value, and "prior restraint" injunctions in First Amendment cases are virtually unknown. This reading of the constitution is supported by decades of jurisprudence, including some recent decisions—for example, a May 2012 ruling by a New York court that struck down a portion of the National Defense Authorization Act that allowed the government to indefinitely detain people suspected of providing "substantial support" for terrorism because of the threat the act posed to free expression.

The sweeping protection generally given to speech in the United States—including speech that many find offensive—is in sharp contrast to legal, political, and social realities in most of the world. As we'll see, many European countries have hate speech laws that explicitly permit censorship of specific types of messages on the ground that they tend to promote unrest, group antagonisms, and sometimes violence. In many countries—including a number in the Middle East—government control of the media means that de facto censorship regimes exist, even when statutes promulgating the notions of "freedom of speech" and "freedom of the press" are on the books.

Ironically, this reality may have helped to exacerbate the angry reactions to *The Innocence of Muslims*. Citizens in the Arab world sometimes extrapolate from the situations in their own countries and conclude that videos, news stories, magazines articles, and books published in the United States must be somehow approved by the government. When they learn about a scurrilous piece of anti-Islam propaganda like *The Innocence of Muslims*, they assume it reflects official U.S. policy.

Comments like "Surely a film like this could never be made if the Obama administration didn't permit it" are widely repeated on the Arab street. The notion that government officials can truly take a neutral, hands-off stance when it comes to regulating speech is difficult for many to grasp.

This misunderstanding of the American tradition of free speech puts our government officials in a difficult spot, as reflected by the confusion and controversy over the administration's responses to the Libyan protests and, ultimately, the deadly violence associated with those protests. Spokespeople for the United States, including the local embassy, State Department officials, and President Obama himself, are all required to transmit a complex, two-sided message: On the one hand, they need to distance themselves from the content of the video and condemn any attempt to deliberately sow hatred and hostility among religious, ethnic, and social groups; on the other, they need to affirm the U.S. commitment to free speech and the right of Americans to produce and distribute materials expressing provocative, inflammatory, and even biased viewpoints. Striking the perfect balance is difficult; in many cases, no one is fully satisfied, as the political controversy over the U.S. response in the *Innocence* case illustrates.

Other messy realities further complicate the story. In the midst of the furor, it was reported—and later confirmed—that an official from the Obama White House contacted YouTube to ask about the inflammatory video. Had its content been vetted by those at the company who are charged with monitoring hateful materials? Had YouTube's own policies regarding hate speech been applied appropriately in this case? The questions undoubtedly heightened YouTube's sense of urgency over the issue and perhaps contributed to the ultimate decision by the service to remove the film from its feed in selected Muslim nations.

This intervention by the White House raised further questions among the public. Did the Obama administration cross some legal or ethical line by making this call? Could a call from the White House be construed as a veiled threat of potential censorship—a subtle sub-version of the First Amendment that seeks to achieve through indirect means what the Constitution directly forbids?

As details emerged, it became clear that the call was an extremely informal contact between a relatively low-level White House employee and a YouTube staffer who happened to be a personal friend, but this fact doesn't necessarily eliminate the concern. It's certainly possible for a government to wield enormous censorship powers through indirect means, including quiet phone calls from government officials asking "friends" in the media to kill particular stories or reports; in some countries, such informal censorship is routine.

The story evolved further in the weeks after the violence when evidence emerged that the attack on the embassy and the murder of the ambassador were not spontaneous responses by an angry crowd but, as we've noted, a deliberately pre-planned terrorist assault that used the film as a mere pretext. Drawing an appropriate balance be-tween the value of free speech and the value of mutual respect and ci-vility is difficult enough. How do we also factor in the possibility that some people—in this case, anti-American terrorists eager to stir up animosity against the United States—may at times go out of their way to take—or at least feign—offense at intemperate rhetoric? Should this possibility lend additional weight to the pro-speech side of the equation, on the ground that those determined to squelch criticism shouldn't be given the power to control the conversation through the use of the "heckler's veto"? Or should it weigh on the side of restraint, on the ground that some speech contributes little or nothing to so-cial enlightenment but merely inflames situations that are already volatile, thereby giving additional power to those whose views are the most extreme and intolerant?

In the case of *The Innocence of Muslims,* the answer is straight-forward. The First Amendment protects the content of the video, no matter how distasteful, and the YouTube terms of service were not obviously violated. If the video had been legally suppressed, it would have created a precedent that could be used to justify censorship of other content that makes important political or social points. Mean-spirited as it was, and notwithstanding the protests it provoked, *The Innocence of Muslims* is not the kind of hate speech that justifies intervention by either government action or Internet hosts.

Yet there is plenty of hate speech online that *does* merit such action. The challenge is how to identify that kind of content and how to respond to it. It's a challenge that those of us who deplore the effects of hate speech on the Internet are bound to try to meet.

HATRED OR HONEST DISSENT? A DELICATE BALANCING ACT

Despite the American tradition of unfettered free speech and our history of civil discourse among dissenting views, there's little agreement among Americans about how threats of violence and unconscionable assaults on human dignity are to be distinguished from mere political dissent.

Consider, for example, the story of Wade M. Page, the troubled military veteran who shocked the nation when he shot and killed worshipers in a Sikh temple in Wisconsin in July 2012.

The 2002 film *Minority Report* is set in a future world in which psychics are able to predict future crimes with pinpoint accuracy and so prevent them. Perhaps fortunately, such mind-reading is impossible in the real world. And yet in a case like that of Wade Page, a handful of advance warning signs of potential violence were visible for all to see. After his discharge from the army in 1998, Page played guitar and sang in several racist rock bands, including two, End Apathy and Definite Hate, that he helped to found. Blue Eyed Devils, another neo-Nazi band that Page joined, sang songs with titles like "White Victory" (sample lyric: "Now I'll fight for my race and nation/Sieg Heil!"). Page wore tattoos linking him to the racist group called the Hammerskins, spoke about attending Hammerfest, an annual white-supremacist festival, and appeared frequently on extremist websites like Stormfront, where he liked to conclude his postings with the code number 88. (Since H is the eighth letter of the alphabet, neo-Nazis use 88 to stand for HH, meaning "Heil Hitler.")[6]

In the world of *Minority Report,* it might have been possible to anticipate and prevent Page's violent future. But in the real world, matters aren't so simple. ADL and the Southern Poverty Law Center (SPLC), which monitor extremist organizations, were both aware of the groups that Page supported and knew his name beginning in 2010. However, neither group saw any definite evidence that Page was capable of an act of racist violence. Page was just one of hundreds of dangerous individuals at the fringes of society who drift in and out of hate groups, leaving traces of their attitudes on webpages and social media sites designed to attract and sometimes inflame others who share the same sense of alienation and anger. There would have been no way to single him out as particularly dangerous before the temple shootings.

Even if the warning flags had been more obvious and threatening, there are still limitations on what society could have done to prevent the potential for violence from becoming a reality. Commenting on the Page case, one federal law enforcement agent said, "We can't launch investigations based on free speech." Paul Bresson of the FBI, which is the leading federal agency responsible for tracking home-grown terror threats, added, "No matter how offensive to some, we are keenly aware that expressing views by itself is not a crime and the protections afforded under the Constitution cannot be compromised."[7]

Political realities complicate the picture still further. In 2009, the Department of Homeland Security (DHS) published a study titled *Rightwing Extremism: Current Economic and Political Climate Fueling*

Resurgence in Radicalization and Recruitment. Written by a team of analysts in the department's intelligence office assigned to study "domestic non-Islamic extremism," the paper noted that the election of the first African American president, together with a deep recession and the resulting atmosphere of social and economic insecurity, had produced a fertile atmosphere for recruitment by right-wing hate groups in the United States. The paper also included a section focusing on "Disgruntled Military Veterans," noting that vets returning from overseas wars with difficult job prospects and intensely honed military skills might be particularly susceptible to the lure of racially or politically motivated violence.

The report provoked a harsh political response. Critics on the right complained that the report was politically motivated, saying it tarred conservatives as potential terrorists and held up military veterans for unfair abuse and demonization. The controversy became so intense that DHS Secretary Janet Napolitano publicly apologized for the report. The intelligence team that produced it was reportedly dissolved, and, according to Daryl Johnson, the leading author of the report, the number of analysts assigned to rightwing extremist groups was sharply reduced. (DHS denied this claim.)

No one would disagree that one of government's crucial roles is to protect citizens from terrorism, no matter its source or motivation. And if such efforts are to be successful, they need to include proactive steps to anticipate and, if possible, discourage or prevent violence rather than merely respond after the fact. Yet the fate of the *Rightwing Extremism* report illustrates how fraught such initiatives are in the United States, thanks in part to our (proper) dedication to freedom of expression, tolerance of a wide range of views, and our current state of political polarization, in which it's increasingly difficult to achieve consensus when it comes to defining hate speech and the appropriate role of government.

WHAT IS HATE SPEECH? DEFINING THE PROBLEM

One key challenge is simply defining hate speech.

Here are some of the categories of speech that could be, and sometimes have been, considered hate speech. As you read the list, you'll almost certainly find yourself nodding in agreement with the use of the term "hate speech" to define some of the items. But you're likely to disagree with it in other cases. And what's more, it's likely that another person chosen at random would agree and disagree at different points than you.

- *Racism*—An article claiming that African Americans are inherently violent, lazy, and stupid; a cartoon depicting President Barack Obama as a baboon; a video saying that black people make up a majority of welfare recipients and are consequently bankrupting the country.
- *Anti-Semitism*—A website that extols Hitler's "Final Solution to the Jewish Problem"; an article supporting the conspiracy theories promulgated in the notorious *Protocols of the Elders of Zion;* a cartoon showing hook-nosed Jewish bankers as vampires sucking the lifeblood out of non-Jewish communities.
- *Religious Bigotry*—An article purporting to "prove" that Mormonism (or Buddhism, Catholicism, Judaism, or some other religion) is actually a "cult" whose secret practices are designed to foment a conspiracy bent on worldwide dominance.
- *Homophobia*—A Facebook page urging readers to "bash in the head of a faggot"; a sermon declaring that gays and lesbians are hated by God and will rot in hell; an article claiming that gays control the media and education and use them to "convert" straight kids.
- *Bigotry Aimed at the Disabled*—A webpage featuring cartoons mocking the blind, the hearing-impaired, and people in

wheelchairs; a site inviting readers to submit jokes about "morons," "imbeciles," and "retards."

- *Political Hatred*—A political blog that denounces another blogger with the words, "Someone ought to put him out of his misery"; a webpage that routinely uses terms like "Nazis," "Commies," "Fascists," "terrorists," and "America-haters" to describe opponents.

- *Rumor-Mongering*—Websites that promote discredited conspiracy theories and phony stories such as "Obama is a Muslim born in Kenya," "Bush planned the 9/11 attacks," "AIDS was deliberately created by the CIA," and "The Holocaust never happened."

- *Misogyny and Violent Pornography*—Images, stories, and statements that promote or excuse violence, degrading treatment, and sexual exploitation aimed against women.

- *Promotion of Terrorism*—Use of the Internet to encourage and spread information about the use of violence for political and social ends, including methods for making bombs and other weapons, techniques for fomenting civil unrest, plots for seizing control of government facilities, and so on.

- *Cyber-Bullying, Harassment, and Stalking*—Use of the Internet, especially social media sites, to humiliate, mock, and attack individuals, urge others to do so, and encourage assaults or suicides.

- *Sale and Promotion of Hate-Oriented Products*—Use of the Internet as an e-commerce platform for selling books, music, videos, games, souvenirs, posters, memorabilia, and other items that promote bigotry, racism, and other forms of hatred.

Do all of these types of materials fall under the broad heading of hate speech? Where would *you* draw the line? And even within a single category, where exactly does the line between "fair speech" and "hate speech" go?

When it comes to crafting such definitions, everyone has his or her sensitive spots. For example, in debating Middle East politics, vicious slanders that challenge the legitimacy of Israel's very existence by playing on age-old stereotypes of Jews as bloody-minded conspirators bent on world domination clearly fall on one side of the line and qualify as hate speech, whereas serious, fair-minded critiques of Israeli government policies clearly fall on the other. But where exactly does the line lie, especially when the statements made and the images conjured up are not as black and white as in the examples we've cited?

In discussions of twentieth-century history, is there a line between Holocaust denial, which claims that the death camps never existed and that Hitler and the Nazis have been unfairly maligned by Jews seeking sympathy for their self-serving agenda, on the one hand, and some form of "historical revisionism" that re-examines accepted theories of the Holocaust in a way that is respectably nuanced and honest, on the other? If so, who would we trust to draw that line?

When it comes to sexual orientation, crude threats directed against "faggots" and fabricated claims that gays and lesbians are seducing underage children as part of an orchestrated campaign to destroy traditional values certainly qualify as homophobic hate speech. But what about arguments against social and political endorsement of same-sex marriage based on religious or social norms? At what point do the rights of particular groups or individuals pass beyond the realm of what is legitimately up for debate?

Most people recognize the anti-black propaganda promulgated by groups like the Ku Klux Klan or the Aryan Nation as out-and-out racism. But what about the racially tinged theories of intelligence that were promoted by scientists like William Shockley? Or the more respectable but still controversial ideas about the genetic inheritance of mental traits found in the writings of scholars like Charles Murray?

If *The Innocence of Muslims* represented anti-Islamic hate speech, what about the 2008 film *Fitna* produced by Geert Wilders, a member of the Dutch House of Parliament, which compared Muslims to Nazis and the Koran to *Mein Kampf?* The controversy over that film caused the Internet web service company Network Solutions to refuse to host it on its servers. It also led to Wilders being barred for a time from entry to the United Kingdom as well as his (ultimately unsuccessful) prosecution by a Dutch court for "incitement to hatred and discrimination." Were these acts of censorship aimed at squelching a legitimate perspective in the name of "political correctness" or appropriate responses to an inflammatory message aimed at promoting hatred for a religion with over a billion adherents around the world?

Disagreements like these are not just matters of theory—they have real-world consequences, occasionally violent ones.

The notion of a single definition of hate speech that everyone can agree on is probably illusory. It's tempting to throw up our hands and echo Justice Potter Stewart's famous definition of pornography: "I know it when I see it." But those of us who take this issue seriously understand that we can't be quite so cavalier. If we want to do something about the problem of hate speech on the Internet, we need to tackle issues of definition head-on.

RESPONDING TO THE CHALLENGE

We can see, then, that defining hate speech in a way that is fair and consistent, and acting to prevent hatemongers from fomenting inter-group hostility and violence, are not simple tasks. In a diverse, complicated world, navigating these choppy waters takes enormous courage, sensitivity, and judgment.

Nonetheless, people of goodwill needn't feel hamstrung and help-less. The First Amendment severely limits what the U.S. government can do to address the problem of hate speech. But the fact that no straightforward legal remedy to hate speech is available does not mean that there is no solution. And the challenge of defining hate speech shouldn't lead us to give up on solving the problem. Instead, we need to work as a society to address the issue directly. There are a number of basic principles that should guide this effort.

First, definitions, practices, principles, and rules governing our policies on hate speech must be developed collaboratively, with par-ticipation by many stakeholders. We'll explain later in this book how such collaborative efforts are already being developed in several quar-ters, and we'll show why we think they are important and worthy of widespread support.

Next, the online companies through which people publish pro-vocative words and images should act judiciously to deal appropriately with their distribution. As private entities, they are not bound by the limitations on government found in the First Amendment. Indeed, it is the First Amendment right of those companies to decide what is in or out of bounds for display on their Internet platforms. While free expression is a value of the highest importance, so too is a civil online environment that respects personal dignity.

Companies like YouTube have a fundamental right to establish and enforce rules governing the kinds of speech that are permissible on their sites. (In a later chapter, we'll discuss in some detail the rules currently in place and their impact on the problem.) But as a practical matter, enforcing such rules is extraordinarily difficult. The sheer volume of content generated by the hundreds of millions of users of YouTube and other social networking sites makes the notion of actively policing that content laughable. (As we write this book, in the fall of 2012, Facebook has announced a new milestone—its one billionth member.)

Thus, enforcement of rules against hate speech on the Internet can only be carried out through the active participation of the users themselves. In effect, the policing of Facebook, YouTube, Twitter, and other online "public squares" must really be self-policing.

At the same time, such "self-policing" is unlikely to happen unless people concerned with online civility and tolerance deliberately band together to make it happen and do so in a way that is consistent, fair, transparent, and unbiased. In much the same way, citizen-run neighborhood safety efforts require organized programs in which trained volunteers work together with law enforcement officials, following clear guidelines as to what forms of intervention are reasonable and appropriate.

Human rights organizations have played an important role in encouraging, designing, and leading such efforts. The impact has been highly positive. We know from our experience at ADL that engaging with the YouTubes of the world to discuss the definition of hate speech and struggling jointly to make fair determinations regarding tricky cases often result in the removal of content that is likely to cause harm. We've seen it happen many times—sometimes even after the corporate gatekeepers have made an initial determination that the content is "in bounds."

For that kind of discussion to happen, people using the Internet—all of us—need to bring hate speech to the attention of the host companies. And that means citizens from every walk of life should be mobilized, educated, and engaged to recognize hate speech, understand the threat it poses, and act to minimize that danger.

Sadly, we live in a world where many of us just assume that hate-filled content, whether videos, websites, or comments to news stories, is an Internet norm. If so, the Internet norm has to change. When we see online hate, we need to *say* something. The sad truth is that a hate-filled video can be just as explosive as a bomb in an abandoned suitcase. Both require our vigilance.

In addition, there's a legitimate role to be played by government officials in monitoring the online activities of violent extremist groups and in educating the public about the dangers they pose. The U.S. government is engaged in such an effort. In February 2013, the White House announced the creation of a new Interagency Working Group to Counter Online Radicalization to Violence, which will coordinate this work. However, there are limits to the role that government can play in this area, as we'll explain in the next chapter.

In the following chapters, we'll discuss in much more detail the steps we can all take to address the dangers posed by hate speech and begin to restore a society where civility and mutual respect are the norm. The challenges of dealing with hate speech are complex, and no purpose would be served by ignoring or minimizing them. But those challenges can be met, and we'll suggest some of the ways forward in the pages to come.

3

"THERE OUGHTA
BE A LAW"

The immediate reaction of many people to the many examples of Internet hate, and to its sometimes fatal but always disturbing effects, is to declare "There oughta be a law." What social purpose is served by words of hate that demonstrably contribute to real-world violence, diminish and insult the dignity of others, mislead and potentially corrupt young people, discourage some people from engaging on the Internet, and generally degrade the medium intended to connect society in beneficial ways? Why not simply forbid hate speech online—through the power of law, if necessary?

Even some Americans who understand our country's commitment to free expression as embodied in the First Amendment to the U.S. Constitution think that the Internet presents a new paradigm, one that requires a re-examination of the traditional boundaries of constitutional law. In short, they think the law should be changed to make it possible for government to regulate, or at least symbolically condemn, hate speech.

Legislatures around the world outside of the United States have responded to this natural assumption. Many countries have passed laws aimed at Internet hate. Many lawmakers see the need to strike a balance between the right to free expression and the right to human dignity—to be free from verbal assaults that could lead to violence or cause emotional distress. In countries where the Holocaust occurred, laws outlawing Holocaust denial and the propagation of Nazi propaganda and imagery have been passed to make it literally unspeakable to deny or revive the Nazi horrors. And even in the United States, existing laws against direct threats or incitements to violence or terrorism at times have been used against online purveyors of hate.

As lawyers steeped in the First Amendment, we know the right to free speech is not absolute, even in the United States. Libel law, copyright law, national security law, and contract limitations all impose legal boundaries on freedom of speech. So it may be surprising that, when we are asked whether we would support new laws limiting hate speech, we respond, "Not necessarily." We might even put it more strongly: In our view, laws addressed at Internet hate are perhaps the *least* effective way to deal with the problem. They create a sense of false security and promote inaction and underuse of other, more powerful tools available to fight online hate.

In this chapter, we'll explain why, and we'll try to show exactly what role we think laws can and should play in the fight against hate speech.

HATE SPEECH AND THE LAW IN THE UNITED STATES

Any discussion of the use of legal remedies in the hate speech arena must begin with a realistic analysis of the current state of the law. There are some law-based tools available to those who want to combat hate speech on the Internet, but there are also deep gaps in legal coverage.

The first crucial distinction is between the United States and other democratic nations. In the United States, the First Amendment to the Constitution guarantees the right of freedom of speech to all Americans, even those whose opinions are reprehensible. As every schoolchild learns—or should learn—the text of the amendment reads, "Congress shall make no law respecting an establishment of religion, or prohibiting the free exercise thereof; or abridging the freedom of speech, or of the press; or the right of the people peaceably to assemble, and to petition the Government for a redress of grievances." Historic court rulings and later amendments, especially the Fourteenth Amendment, confirmed that the same restrictions apply to other governmental bodies at all levels, including state and local governments.

It would be a mistake to take the seemingly absolute terms of the First Amendment too literally. Despite the apparent blanket prohibition embodied in the bald words "no law," courts and legislatures have always recognized that some forms of speech can be appropriately limited or regulated through the actions of government and the legal system. For example, the First Amendment does not protect the use of language to commit fraud, libel or slander an individual, violate others' intellectual property rights, or foment criminal conspiracies.

Furthermore, people acting in specific roles and specific public settings can have their speech legally regulated. Attorneys and judges, for instance, may be sanctioned for intemperate or hateful statements in a court of law, prison guards may be punished for verbally abusing prisoners, and public school teachers may be restricted in the messages they communicate in the classroom.[1] Even though these limitations on free speech may be imposed by government action, they're not regarded as violations of the guarantees in the First Amendment.

Nonetheless, it is broadly correct to say that the United States provides very robust protection to most forms of public expression, erecting high barriers intended to prevent government from regulating speech on the basis of its content. And while most people consider hate speech a particularly odious form of speech, the U.S. Supreme Court has made clear that First Amendment protections usually extend to such speech. Yes, there are exceptions, which we'll explain in the next few pages. But these exceptions are narrowly drawn and strictly defined. Unless the speech contains a direct, credible, "true" threat against an identifiable individual, organization, or institution; is libelous; meets the legal test for harassment; or constitutes incitement to imminent lawless action likely to occur, little recourse against hate speech will be available under American law.

These tests apply to online speech in the same way as they do to communications in any other forum. In a number of recent decisions, the Supreme Court has reaffirmed that our government may not regulate the content of Internet speech to any greater extent than it may regulate speech in more traditional areas of expression, such as the print media, the broadcast media, or the public square. While courts may take into account the Internet's vast reach and accessibility when evaluating the impact of particular forms of speech, they must still approach attempts to censor or regulate speech online from a traditional constitutional framework. That means beginning with the assumption that freedom of speech is a paramount value that can only be abridged in specific, carefully defined circumstances.

U.S. courts have been reluctant to make an exception with regard to expressions of hate speech. Consider, for example, the historic 1977 case *National Socialist Party of America v. Village of Skokie,* in which the U.S. Supreme Court allowed a "Nazi parade" to march through the streets of a predominantly Jewish town.[2] The court later confirmed its reluctance to permit regulation of hate speech when it struck down a Minnesota city ordinance banning speech that "arouses anger, alarm or resentment in others on the basis of race, color, creed, religion, or gender." In that case, the Supreme Court noted that it cannot permit a government to impose special prohibitions on those who express disfavored views.

Likewise, the concept of "group libel"—hateful comments directed toward Jews, blacks, or any other religious or racial group— cannot be used as a weapon against bigots who spew invective online or off. The courts have repeatedly held that libel directed against religious or racial groups does not create an actionable offensive. (Libel on the Internet directed toward a particular person or entity, of course, is actionable under the law just like libelous remarks uttered in any public forum.)

So hate speech, in general, is protected by the broad umbrella of our First Amendment. However, there are a number of specific exceptions. Let's consider these, one by one.

Threats and Intimidation

There may be legal remedies available when hate speech crosses the line into threats and intimidation. Under the law, threats are not protected under the First Amendment. This applies to threats involving racial epithets and those motivated by racial animus. Thus, a threatening private message sent over the Internet to a victim, or even a public message displayed on a website describing intent to commit acts of racially motivated violence, can be prosecuted under the law. Generally defined as declarations of "intention to inflict punishment, loss, or pain on another, or to injure another by the commission of some unlawful act," such "true threats" receive no First Amendment protection.[3] Thus, a threatening email or comment posting on a website that conveys an intention to commit acts of racially motivated violence and specifically identifiable people could be lawfully punished.

Notice that, in order to be legally actionable, threats must be "true." Under an objective test employed by some courts, a reasonable person must foresee that the statement would be interpreted by the recipient as a serious expression of intent to harm or assault. To establish a "true threat," some courts have held that the government must prove that the maker of the threat reasonably should have foreseen that the statement he uttered would be taken as a threat by those to whom it was made. So, for example, a trial court held that it was legally permissible to try someone who had, among other things, emailed a college dean saying, "You will die soon, mother f****r. But you will watch your son die first," as well as emailing a professor with the words, "You are on the death list!"[4]

In another case, *U.S. v. Voneida,* the U.S. Court of Appeals for the Third Circuit upheld the conviction of a university student who had posted threats to others on a social media page two days after the shootings at Virginia Tech.[5] The student had posted several statements and pictures to his MySpace page, including a number of violent statements, such as, "Someday: I'll make the Virginia Tech incident look like a trip to an amusement park," and captioning a posting, "Virginia Tech Massacre—They got what they deserved." The student noted that his current mood was "extatically [*sic*] happy" and included a poem dedicated to the Virginia Tech shooter in which he concluded that the shooter's "undaunted and unquenched" wrath would "sweep across the land."

Because fellow students were on his MySpace "buddy" list, the poster was considered to have made and delivered a threat. The court further noted that "While some of the statements, taken in isolation, may not rise to the level of a threat within the meaning of § 875(c), that was not the context of the case here." Hate speech, then, can be prosecuted under U.S. law when it crosses the line from mere expression of contempt or hatred into a "true threat" of intention to harm another.

Advocacy of Violence

Speech that contains an incitement to imminent violence—even when not a direct threat—may also fall outside the protection of the First Amendment. Note, however, that the First Amendment has been held to protect speech that advocates violence, so long as the speech is not directed to inciting or producing imminent lawless action and is not likely to incite or produce such action.[6] This means, for example, that individuals can freely propose violent reactions to contemporary problems or threaten menacing actions unless their words are actually likely to result in violence and the violence is likely to occur imminently. This so-called Brandenburg standard (named after the Supreme Court case that established it) sets a very high bar. Online hate speech will rarely be punishable in court under this test.

The leading case that sought to establish the line with respect to online hate speech involved Neal Horsley, an anti-abortion activist who used information provided by the American Coalition of Life Activists (ACLA) to create an anti-abortion website known as the Nuremberg Files.[7] The site offered extensive personal information about some 200 abortion providers: pictures, addresses, phone numbers, license-plate numbers, Social Security numbers, and names and birth dates of spouses and children. Viewers were exhorted to send photos, video-tapes, and data on "the abortionist, their car, their house, friends, and anything else of interest." The site said that the information garnered would be used to prosecute abortion providers at some time in the future when abortion becomes illegal, just as Nazi leaders were pros-ecuted after World War II—hence the "Nuremberg" label.

Most disturbing, the list of abortion providers at the Nuremberg Files site read like a list of targets for assassination. Names listed in plain black lettering were of doctors still "working," those printed in "greyed-out" letters were "wounded," and those names that were crossed out ("strike-through") indicated doctors who had been murdered ("fatality"). The implication seemed clear to most outside observers: Horsley was indi-rectly recommending that visitors to the website take it upon themselves to seek out and murder doctors who were performing abortions.

The Nuremberg Files trial court wrestled with the issue of whether the website constituted protected speech under the First Amendment or qualified as a "true threat." At trial, the jury found that the ACLA website was a threat to plaintiffs and ordered the website owners and operators to pay plaintiffs over $100 million in damages. The court then issued a permanent injunction to prevent the defendants from providing additional information to the Nuremberg Files website.

However, the story didn't end there. The Appellate Court unanimously reversed, holding that the defendants' website was a lawful expression of views protected by the First Amendment. On appeal, the court concluded that "unless [defendants] threatened that its members would themselves assault the doctors, the First Amendment protects its speech." The court later decided to rehear the case *en banc* and in an 8–3 decision held that the website constituted a true "threat of force" and was *not* protected by the First Amendment. Thus, the Appellate ruling found that a true threat, that is, one where a reasonable person would foresee that a reader would believe himself to be subject to physical violence upon his person, is unprotected under the First Amendment.

Responding to arguments made by the American Civil Liberties Union as a "friend of the court," the Appellate Court stated that it is not necessary for the defendant to intend to or be able to carry out his threat. Rather, "[t]he only intent requirement is that the defendant intentionally or knowingly communicate the threat." "The Nuremberg Files go beyond merely offensive or provocative speech. . . . As a result, we cannot say that it is clear as a matter of law . . . [these] are purely protected, political speech."

Thus, after the Nuremberg Files case, it appears that hateful content, when it knowingly and intentionally communicates a credible threat, will not be protected by U.S. courts. But drawing the line can be a difficult matter, as the complex history of the Nuremberg Files case underscores.

Harassment

Similarly, harassing speech—speech that inflicts or intends to inflict emotional or physical harm, and that is persistent enough to amount to a "course of conduct" rather than an isolated incident—is not constitutionally protected. Thus, targeting an individual with harassing speech is not a constitutionally protected activity under U.S. law when the speech in question amounts to impermissible conduct.

But when, exactly, does speech cross the line from being "mere speech" to being an impermissible "course of conduct"? According to court rulings, in order for speech to be considered harassing, it must be persistent and pernicious and must inflict significant emotional or physical harm. Furthermore, harassment, like threats, must be directed at specific individuals. Blanket statements expressing hatred of an ethnic, racial, or religious group in general cannot be considered harassment, even if those statements distress individual members of that ethnic group. However, if a person continually directs racist statements at a single victim, such speech may rise to the level of harassment even if the racist remarks do not specifically mention the victim.

Speech that meets these criteria is viewed as a form of impermissible conduct, not just speech. Harassing online speech may be actionable as cyber-bullying or under workplace anti-harassment laws.

Hate Speech and the War on Terror

Historically, America's commitment to free speech has been most severely tested in times of national crisis or war. The ongoing War on Terror constitutes the latest such test. After September 11th, people across the globe were forced to acknowledge the significant threat posed by Muslim extremists. They also recognized the important role the Internet has played in developing and carrying out this threat. Al-Qaeda operatives relied heavily on the Internet in planning and coordinating the September 11th attacks.

More broadly, supporters of Osama bin Laden and Al-Qaeda have openly acknowledged the power of the Internet as a propaganda tool. For instance, the website of Azzam Publications, a British publisher accused of selling materials in support of terrorism, stated that "due to the advances of modern technology it is easy to spread news, information, articles and other information over the internet. We strongly urge Muslim Internet professionals to spread and disseminate news and information about the Jihad though e-mail lists, discussion groups, and their own Websites. If you fail to do this, and our site closes down before you have done this, we may hold you to account before Allah on the Day of Judgment."[8] (The Azzam Publications site closed down shortly after September 11th.)

It seems logical that communications designed to assist in the performance of acts of terror should forfeit the protection of the First Amendment. But as always when complex matters of law are involved, the devil is in the details. It is easy to understand why the prosecution of credible threats aimed at targeted groups has been successful. In other instances, however, the precise connection between the message and the messenger may not be so clear. What if the defendant merely facilitated the spread of hate by providing technical assistance and creating web pages, but did not provide content?

Where should courts draw the line? In the aftermath of the September 11th attacks, the Sami Al-Hussayen case tested those limits.

Thirty-four-year-old Saudi national Sami Al-Hussayen, a computer science doctoral candidate at the University of Idaho, was accused by the U.S. government of supporting terrorism by using his online skills to create an Internet network that financed and recruited terrorists. Al-Hussayen was accused of allegedly conspiring with the Islamic Assembly of North America (IANA) to support terrorism by operating and maintaining a radical Islamic website. For example, one of the websites registered by Al-Hussayen on September 11, 2000 (www.alasr.ws), published an article titled "Provision of Suicide Operations." Written by a radical Saudi sheikh, the article included language explaining why a *Mujahid* (warrior) must kill himself if this can produce the death of a large number of "enemies," and it explained in detail how this can be accomplished.

The United States argued that Al-Hussayen's websites contained content so subversive that it convinced people to finance terrorism or become part of it. Under the Patriot Act, enacted one month after September 11th, a person within the United States or subject to the jurisdiction thereof who knowingly provides material support or resources to a foreign terrorist organization, or attempts to conspire to do so, which includes expert advice or assistance, may be prosecuted for conspiracy to support terrorism and imprisoned for up to fifteen years. The Act itself provided for no First Amendment exception; thus, even when assistance counts as free speech or free association, it still may fall within the Act.

Yet in the end, the jury voted unanimously after just three hours of deliberation to acquit Al-Hussayen, demonstrating the limits of government power over Internet content, even in the post-September 11th era. One juror, a retired federal employee named John Steger, suggested that the prosecution had gone too far in this case. "There was not a word spoken that indicated [Al-Hussayen] supported terrorism," said Steger. "It was a real stretch."[9]

The War on Terror may have tested Americans' commitment to the principle of freedom of speech—but if the Al-Hussayen case is any indication, that commitment remains fundamentally intact.

Hate Speech As Evidence of Hate Crime

While hate speech online is not in itself punishable in the United States, it may provide evidence of motive in a hate crime case. Hate crime laws typically work by increasing a criminal's sentence if the prosecution can prove that the criminal intentionally selected a victim based on the victim's real or perceived race, nationality, religion, gender, or sexual orientation. If online hate speech rises to the level of criminal conduct, it may subject the perpetrator to an enhanced sentence under a state's hate crimes law. Hate speech, alone, with no underlying criminal conduct, would not be subject to hate crime laws.

Forty-five states and the District of Columbia currently have some form of hate crime law on the books that enables prosecutors to seek increased penalties when a victim is targeted in a bias crime. (ADL has long been a strong supporter of hate crime laws, and it has worked closely with legislators to help design effective statutes in this area. For more information on this, see Appendix F.) When hate speech on the Internet inspires violence, evidence about that speech could aid the prosecution in seeking an increased penalty under an applicable hate crimes statute.

While this concept, as of fall 2012, has only been applied to hate speech found in movies, there have been an increasing number of crimes committed by perpetrators who read hate literature online. For example, as we discussed in chapter one, the racially motivated shooting of blacks, Asian Americans, and Jews in suburban Chicago over the 1999 Fourth of July weekend was carried out by a member of World Church of the Creator, Benjamin Nathaniel Smith, who, according to law enforcement officials, admitted to reading hate literature online. There have been similar cases where perpetrators of hate crimes have found inspiration in literature that is easily obtainable on the Internet. It seems reasonable to assume that, eventually, one or more cases will be prosecuted in which hate speech from the Internet will help to establish the hate-driven motive of a criminal and thereby assist in obtaining a hate crime conviction.

The Limits of the Law

As our brief review of the law regarding hate speech has suggested, there are narrow limits as to the kinds of speech that government is permitted to control through the use of law. These limits place online hate speech largely beyond the reach of law.

There are also practical limitations to what law can do about online hate speech. The anonymity of the Internet makes it difficult to track down and prosecute perpetrators of threatening messages. This proved true in a recent case involving a Detroit boy who received a barrage of anti-Semitic death threats in his email inbox. The eleven-year-old immediately reported the incident to his parents, who notified the local police. Investigators discovered that the boy had innocently stumbled on a hater while surfing through a public chat area on the web. They tried to identify the perpetrator, but the investigation turned up few clues as to the source of the anonymous threats. Eventually, it was determined that the source was disguised, quite possibly outside of the country, and well beyond the reach of local authorities. It's likely that many cases of threats or harassment over the Internet would prove hard to prosecute because of practical difficulties like these.

Nonetheless, there have been some successful prosecutions of senders of hate mail. In 1998, a student at the University of California, Irvine, transmitted a threatening email to Asian students in which he promised to "make it my life career to find and kill everyone one [sic] of you personally." The student was caught and convicted of a civil rights violation. He was sentenced to a year in prison. There have been other similar convictions.

And where an individual or identifiable group is targeted for harm, it's clear that the government has the power to step in. For example, the website of neo-Nazi Bill White, which posted the address of Ottawa-based civil rights lawyer Richard Warman and urged readers to take violent action against him, is plainly illegal in the United States. (It is a travesty that the Canadian Radio-Television and Telecommunications Commission [CRTC] could not fashion an immediate legal remedy to force the removal of this threat from White's website.) In at least one U.S. jurisdiction, covering California and much of the West, the highest appellate court—the Ninth Circuit—has ruled that specific threats like that addressed to Mr. Warman justify an injunction shutting down the website containing the threats, as well as millions of dollars in damages. And that is the right result.

HATE SPEECH LAWS AROUND THE WORLD

As we've seen, in the United States, the traditional protection of the First Amendment establishes strict limits on the degree to which the government can prosecute hateful speech in any form, including on-line. What about in other countries that lack America's constitutional legacy? There the story is quite different. In a number of countries, legal action to express society's outrage against hate speech is legally feasible to a far greater extent than in the United States. The underlying laws, however, are quite varied, as even a cursory review will show.

In Denmark, for example, Article 266b of the Penal Code reads, in part, "Whoever publicly, or with intention to disseminating in a larger circle, makes statements or other pronouncements, by which a group of persons is threatened, derided or degraded because of their race, colour of skin, national or ethnic background, faith or sexual orientation, will be punished by fine or imprisonment for up to two years." In this law, the key concept appears to be the "threatening, deriding, or degrading" of a group of people by the message in question.

In the United Kingdom, Section 18(1) of Public Order Act 1986 states, "A person who uses threatening, abusive or insulting words or behaviour, or displays any written material which is threatening, abusive or insulting, is guilty of an offence if—(a) he intends thereby to stir up racial hatred, or (b) having regard to all the circumstances racial hatred is likely to be stirred up thereby." By contrast with the Danish law, this law emphasizes the intention of the speaker or publisher to stir up racial hatred, or the likelihood that such hatred will be stirred up—a test that the Danish law doesn't impose.

In New Zealand, Section 61(1) of the 1993 Human Rights Act says, "It shall be unlawful for any person—(a) To publish or distribute written matter which is threatening, abusive, or insulting, or to broadcast by means of radio or television words which are threatening, abusive, or insulting; or (b) To use in any public place as defined in section 2(1) of the Summary Offences Act 1981, or within the hearing of persons in any such public place, or at any meeting to which the public are invited or have access, words which are threatening, abusive, or insulting; or (c) To use in any place words which are threatening, abusive, or insulting if the person using the words knew or ought to have known that the words were reasonably likely to be published in a newspaper, magazine, or periodical or broadcast by means of radio or television,—being matter or words likely to excite hostility against or bring into contempt any group of persons in or who may be coming to New Zealand on the ground of the colour, race, or ethnic or national origins of that group of persons." Among other differences, this New Zealand law specifically refers to groups of people who are in the country or may be coming to the country, and it limits its coverage to messages related to "colour, race, or ethnic or national origins," whereas the Danish law also includes "faith or sexual orientation." (The British law, as you've probably noticed, mentions only "racial hatred," though other laws in the United Kingdom do address sexual orientation, religion, and other grounds for hatred.)

Comparable laws exist in other countries, each with its local distinctions. For example, in Austria, Belgium, Czech Republic, France, Germany, Hungary, Romania, Poland, and Luxembourg, laws against Holocaust denial send a message to all citizens (especially impressionable children) that it is literally unspeakable to lie about history given the horrors of genocide inflicted in those countries during the twentieth century. The many significant differences among the hate speech laws found in countries around the world make it obvious that there is no such thing as a "universal standard" for prosecuting hate speech—even when the sharply contrasting example of the United States is excluded from the conversation.

This brief overview, however, makes it obvious that other democracies take a different approach to hate speech than the United States. The sense shared by many Americans that freedom of speech and of the press are (almost) absolute rights is absent in Europe and elsewhere; the willingness to proscribe specific forms of speech because of their content is far greater elsewhere than in the United States.

But even in the absence of a First Amendment right to free speech, hate speech laws in the other global democracies have not gone unchallenged. As you might expect, extremist groups that would like to enjoy the freedom to disseminate bigoted messages have protested hate speech laws. But so have some journalists, authors, publishers, and free speech advocates, who worry about how hate speech laws might be abused in the hands of despotic or simply short-sighted governments. History shows that the temptation to use government power to silence political opposition is a powerful one. Conscious of this danger, proponents of civil liberties have pushed back against the existence of hate speech laws in many democratic countries.

In Canada, one of the most controversial legal bulwarks against hate speech was eliminated in June 2012, with the repeal of Section 13 of the Human Rights Act. Under the provisions of Section 13, originally enacted in 1999, using telecommunications facilities (including the Internet) to communicate "any matter that is likely to expose a person or persons to hatred or contempt by reason of the fact that that person or those persons are identifiable on the basis of a prohibited ground of discrimination" was a "discriminatory practice." Those "prohibited grounds" included race, religion, and sexual orientation. The law authorized government human rights tribunals to monitor such content and, when they deemed it appropriate, to levy financial penalties against the publishers of forbidden content.

The law was undoubtedly well intentioned, and many supported it. But many others considered it overly broad and decried its chilling effect on free debate. Alan Borovoy, general counsel for the Canadian Civil Liberties Association, pointed to some questionable applications of Section 13 in calling for its repeal:

> Although it's true that they have nailed some genuine hatemongers with it, it has nevertheless been used or threatened to be used against a wide variety of constituencies who don't bear the slightest resemblance to the kind of hatemongers that were originally envisioned: anti-American protesters, French-Canadian nationalists, a film sympathetic to South Africa's Nelson Mandela, a pro-Zionist book, a Jewish community leader, Salman Rushdie's *Satanic Verses*, and even a couple years ago, a pro-Israeli speaker was briefed about the anti-hate law by a police detective before he went in to make a speech.[10]

By 2012, the critics had commanded a majority in the House of Commons, and Section 13 was repealed. However, a different law—Section 319(1) of the Canadian Criminal Code—remains available as a weapon in the fight against hate speech. It reads, in part, "Everyone who, by communicating statements in any public place, incites hatred against any identifiable group where such incitement is likely to lead to a breach of the peace is guilty of . . . an indictable offence and is liable to imprisonment for a term not exceeding two years." Similar statutes exist in some Canadian provinces.

SHOULD THE UNITED STATES OUTLAW HATE SPEECH?

So far, we've devoted this chapter to explaining the current legal land-scape regarding hate speech—the laws and practices that are actually in place in the United States and elsewhere in the world. But what role *should* the law play in addressing the problem of online hate? Is the American fixation on the supremacy of the First Amendment still valid in an age when incitements to group hatred can go viral, infecting thousands of millions of people overnight and potentially sparking disastrous social consequences? Should the United States consider following the lead of other democratic nations and carve out a large exception to the First Amendment by permitting laws that actually forbid hate speech?

There's a body of respectable opinion that advocates this position. Jeremy Waldron, a gifted legal thinker and a thoughtful social critic, defends this stance in his 2012 book *The Harm in Hate Speech*. Waldron endorses the concept of "group libel," noting that even the name of the Anti-Defamation League contains a suggestion that groups, not just individuals, can indeed be libeled, defamed, or slandered by the publication of vicious untruths about them.[11] Waldron suggests that "group defamation" or "group libel" laws are useful "to vindicate public order, not just by preempting violence, but by upholding against attack a shared sense of the basic elements of each person's status, dignity, and reputation as a citizen or member of society in good standing."[12]

Waldron goes on to discuss, quite eloquently, the ideal of a "well-ordered society" as including a modicum of respect for every member of that society as reflected in the public sphere. And he contends that laws prohibiting extreme expressions of disdain for particular groups—expressions that provoke attitudes of hatred, rejection, and contempt—are defensible in pursuit of that ideal.

It could also be argued that the United States is actually already obligated by international agreements to take legal action against hate speech. For example, the International Covenant on Civil and Political Rights (ICCPR), signed by 167 nations including the United States, sets standards for recognition of human rights. It includes a provision in article 20(2) that states that "Any advocacy of national, racial or religious hatred that constitutes incitement to discrimination, hostility or violence shall be prohibited by law." Such prohibition would go beyond the current standard interpretation of the First Amendment by U.S. courts. ("Incitement to violence," as we've seen, can be prohibited in the United States, but not mere "incitement to discrimination" or "hostility.")

Note that the provisions of the ICCPR do not in themselves render hate speech "illegal" in any country; they merely bind the signatory nations to create laws that would have this effect. Thus, the ICCPR is not "self-enforcing" but requires further action to go into effect. More significant, when the U.S. Senate ratified the treaty in 1992, it did so subject to a number of "reservations, declarations, and understandings," including, most important, this one: "Nothing in this Covenant requires or authorizes legislation, or other action, by the United States of America prohibited by the Constitution of the United States as interpreted by the United States." (Similarly, when ratifying the 2001 Budapest Convention on Cybercrime, the U.S. Senate expressly refused to ratify the hate speech protocol included in that convention.)

Some critics have complained that reservations like these have rendered the American ratification of the ICCPR practically meaningless. That may be going too far. But it is true that this international accord, along with some others that contain similar provisions, has had little or no real impact on U.S. jurisprudence, political views, or public attitudes.

Most Americans may despise hate speech, but they also agree that they don't want to outlaw it, regardless of what people in other countries do. For example, a Rasmussen poll conducted in 2008 asked American adults whether it would be "a good idea for the United States to ban hate speech." Twenty-eight percent of respondents said yes, while fifty-three percent said no. A follow-up question, worded differently, produced even more lopsided results. When asked, "Which is better—allowing free speech without government interference or letting government decide what types of hate speech should be banned?" only eleven percent chose government intervention, while seventy-four percent said they preferred unfettered free speech.[13] Other surveys have shown similar results.

This conviction isn't merely an outgrowth of the enshrinement of freedom of speech in our First Amendment, which many consider the single most important bulwark of freedom in American democracy. It's also a reflection of a pluralistic, multi-ethnic, continually evolving society in which vigorous, ever-shifting debates about public policy have always been a prominent feature of the political and social landscape. Historically, the United States has been a country in which slave owners and abolitionists, "robber barons" and socialists, pacifists and saber-rattlers, prohibitionists and anti-prohibitionists, gun rights defenders and would-be gun banners, and pro-life activists and pro-choice activists have all shared the debating platform, the airwaves, the courthouse, and the halls of government, arguing their diverse points of view with intensity and sometimes incivility. Americans are accustomed to such debates (although at election times we sometimes become a bit weary of them), and we consider them an essential element in the long-term quest for truth. Accordingly, we look askance at attempts to stifle debate and are willing to tolerate a greater degree of rancor than citizens of some other countries.

Furthermore, there are legitimate grounds for worry that hate speech laws can be abused for political reasons by those in power or by groups defending their own sensibilities. History points to worrisome examples. India's penal code, for example, contains a well-intentioned prohibition against messages that "outrage religious feelings"—an understandable principle in a society where varying faiths have lived together for thousands of years. But the rule has been used by extremist Hindu groups to mount a series of costly lawsuits against the painter M. F. Husain, widely regarded as India's greatest modern artist, on the ground that his nude depictions of Hindu gods and goddesses constituted an affront to their religion. Husain ultimately fled his homeland to escape this legal persecution.[14]

Western countries, including the United States, have experienced similar problems. Columbia Law School's Jamal Greene notes:

> Hate-speech restrictions in particular have a history of missing their originally intended marks. New Jersey's 1935 race-hate statute, born of violent confrontations between Nazi sympathizers and their antagonists, was used only against a group of Jehovah's Witnesses before the New Jersey Supreme Court declared the law unconstitutional in 1941. In Great Britain, the Public Order Act 1936, enacted in response to the fascist threat, was used against Bertrand Russell and other antinuclear protesters in 1961.[15]

Americans instinctively understand that laws restricting speech based primarily on its content are inherently dangerous—weapons ready to be grabbed and used in the heat of crisis by anyone seeking to shut down public debate for whatever reason. This danger isn't an insurmountable argument against hate speech laws, but it's a very important one that American courts have rightly taken seriously.

DO HATE SPEECH LAWS WORK?

These, then, are some of the legal, social, and political arguments for and against the enactment of laws regulating hate speech. But what about the practical considerations? Do hate speech laws work? Are they an effective tool for a society to wield in its efforts to create and maintain a civil, respectful, and mutually tolerant public sphere?

There are many who believe that prosecutions such as that of David Irving (the notorious "historian" whose writings express sympathy for the Nazis and minimize the significance of the Holocaust) do more to promote visibility and stir up benighted supporters than they do to quell future hate speech and enlighten the public. As columnist Michael Moynihan has observed:

> [J]ailing pseudo-historians for arguing against historical fact creates martyrs: Why do we know the names of David Irving, Robert Faurisson, Bishop Richard Williamson, and Ernst Zundel and not those who have denied the Cambodian genocide, or those who claim that the Srebrenica massacre was fabricated or that the 9/11 attacks were an Israeli-sponsored "inside job"? (Such anti-Israel conspiracy theories are not illegal in Europe, despite being marinated in anti-Semitic paranoia about omnipotent Jewish power.) It's partially because we know victims of the Holocaust and their relatives—those [Nobel Laureate Elie] Wiesel understandably wants to protect from psychological injury. And it's because of those postwar Germans who said *nie wieder,* insisting that their country grapple with its past by requiring the study of the Holocaust in school curricula.
>
> But we also know their names because Irving, Faurisson, and Zundel have been hauled before courts in France, Germany, and Austria to face criminal charges. Earlier this year, Iranian President Mahmoud Ahmadinejad garlanded Faurisson with an award for his "courage, strength,

and force" against the Jewish enemy. This is the result of failing to trust regular people to adjudicate historical truth; Europe has inadvertently elevated liars.[16]

Thus, like many laws, hate speech statutes may have unintended consequences, including the creation of "martyrs" around whom hate-mongers can rally when their ideas are legally stifled.

Furthermore, the reflexive use of the law as the tool of first resort to deal with online hate speech threatens to weaken respect for the law if such attempted law enforcement fails or is used against minor violations. For example, consider the 2000 case (*LICRA v. Yahoo!*) brought to enforce the French law that prohibits the selling or display of neo-Nazi memorabilia. The case was brought with respect to online sales by third-party users of the Yahoo! service. It led to extended international litigation over whether the French could proceed against the Yahoo.com site—its U.S. domain—as well as the local Yahoo.fr domain, illustrating the complexity of attempts by individual nation-states to control the inherently global content of the Internet. In the end, Yahoo! voluntarily agreed to adopt a rule restricting third parties from selling or displaying Nazi memorabilia. Yet critics wonder how meaningful this victory was. Even in 2000, the Internet contained plenty of pro-Nazi content that was far more offensive and disturbing than the memorabilia sales sites, and the focus on the marketing of Nazi trinkets may have served merely to trivialize the speech codes directed at Holocaust deniers and neo-Nazis.

There are also severe practical limitations on the power of law to control online hate. Even if law enforcement officers wanted to monitor online content and attempt to remove anything that promoted hatred, it would be physically impossible. It's simply impossible to monitor and police the vast proliferation of bigoted content being distributed through Web 2.0 technologies. For every take-down of offensive content, new content multiplies. As noted by Jeremy Waldron—who, as we have seen, is actually an advocate of legal efforts to control hate speech—"By and large, the law has to rely in this area—as in almost every area—on self-application by ordinary citizens. And this means that any citizen who relies upon the *law* is, in the last analysis, relying indirectly on the voluntary cooperation of his or her fellow citizens."[17]

Moreover, given that the United States, with its First Amendment, is essentially a safe haven for virtually all Web content, removing content or shutting down a website in Europe or Canada through legal channels is far from a guarantee that the contents have been censored for all time.

The borderless nature of the Internet means that, like chasing cockroaches, squashing one offending website, page, or service provider does not solve the problem; there are many more waiting behind the walls—or across the border. Prosecution of Internet speech in one country is a futile gesture when the speech can re-appear on the Internet almost instantaneously, hosted by an Internet service provider (ISP) in the United States.

Some argue that, despite these weaknesses, hate speech laws play an important "expressive" role in society, serving as powerful symbols of public condemnation of bigotry. There's truth to this assertion. The German prosecutions of notorious anti-Semites and Holocaust deniers Ernst Zundel and Frederick Toeben expressed society's outrage at the messages and warned people who spread hate that they may well go to jail for their actions. But all you need to do is insert the names of those criminals into a Google search and you will find websites of supporters paying homage to them as martyrs and republishing their messages.

Furthermore, not all laws that seek to regulate speech in the name of civility and social harmony are created equal—and not all deserve equal support from the world community. Cross-border prosecutions of international hate speech offenders could give support to repressive regimes. For example, China could request international support and assistance in enforcing their own speech laws, which they liken to the laws prohibiting Holocaust denial but in fact are laws squelching the free expression of ideas. Defining the acceptable limits of free speech for legal purposes is not a simple matter, especially when international social and political standards come into play.

Clearly, then, the legal issues surrounding hate speech on the Internet are complicated and still evolving, especially on the international scale. What conclusions can be drawn by those of us who want to take action to prevent the further spread of online hate?

Our view is that countries with speech codes should use extreme discretion in enforcing those laws against Internet hate speech, lest the enforcement be seen as ineffectual, resulting in a diminished respect for the law. It's also important to recognize that the realities of the Internet are such that with Web 2.0 viral technologies, removing comments or a video or shutting down a website through legal means in one country is far from a guarantee that the website is shuttered for all time. Certainly in absolute terms, new laws have not stemmed the tide of new websites and social networking sites containing hate speech.

This is not to say that the law should be discarded as a tool. But it should be regarded more as a silver bullet, reserved for egregious offenders where the outcome of an exemplary case can make a meaningful difference, rather than as a shotgun, scattering pellets in the direction of a vast set of targets and having marginal effect.

Thus, the law is but one tool in the fight against online hate—and not, in our judgment, the most powerful one. "There oughta be a law"? Maybe. But there are better ways of tackling the problem of online hatred—and in the next chapter, we'll examine some of them.

HATE SPEECH AND THE GATEKEEPERS OF THE INTERNET

As we've seen, the law is a relatively weak tool when it comes to dealing with hate speech. Constitutional, political, social, and technical factors work together to ensure that governments have limited power to control the content of the Internet. In many ways, this is a good thing. The Internet has already been, and will likely continue to be, a force for democratization around the world, thanks in large part to the inability of despotic regimes to suppress its use by free people. Yet for the same reasons, those with questionable motives—including purveyors of hate—are free to use the Internet to spread lies, threats, and hostility.

But what about the corporate entities that manage, and profit from, vast swaths of the Internet? The businesses that host websites, stream content, organize social media, and maintain connections among individuals and organizations around the globe have a much more direct and intimate connection to Internet users and to the content they create than governments do. What responsibilities do they have concerning the use, or abuse, of their services by hatemongers? And how well are they meeting their social obligations as powerful corporate citizens?

Let's begin the discussion by addressing a common misunderstanding. As we've seen, in the United States, the First Amendment to the Constitution mandates strict limits to the power of government to control speech. Over more than two centuries of history, our respect for the Bill of Rights has gradually given rise to a widespread cultural norm in favor of unfettered communication in almost every medium—so much so that many people assume that *any* limits on free speech are legally and constitutionally forbidden. Thus, when private entities such as television networks, publishers, or corporate employers choose to limit a particular form of expression because they disapprove of its content, they can expect to be widely criticized: "They can't do that, can they? That's censorship! It's against the First Amendment!"

This is a fundamental mistake. The Constitution, including the First Amendment, is a blueprint for the organization and operation of American government; its rules restrict what national, state, and local government agencies can do, not what private individuals or organizations can do. Thus, "freedom of speech" or "freedom of the press" doesn't mean that everyone is entitled to access broadcast time, columns of newsprint, or a page on a website—that access is granted through private entities, which have the right (and the responsibility) to make their own decisions about what to broadcast, publish, or otherwise disseminate.

So when a private business, such as CBS, the *New York Times,* or the *Huffington Post,* chooses to promote and publicize one set of messages and reject another, it is perfectly within its rights to do so—and "censorship," which is, strictly speaking, a matter of government action, doesn't factor into the equation. (Of course, anyone is free to criticize the editorial judgments made by these private organizations, and many do. But the judgments are theirs to make.)

Now, most of these private companies in the media industries recognize that they have dual responsibilities. On the one hand, as for-profit businesses (which most of them are), they have a responsibility to their owners (such as shareholders) to turn a profit—which requires them to attract widespread interest in their offerings so as to generate revenue, whether through newspaper or magazine purchases, sales of advertising space, online shopping commissions, or other methods. This financial responsibility means that most media companies are interested in pursuing popularity—publishing materials that audiences will find attractive, compelling, and fascinating.

On the other hand, managers at most media companies also accept that they have a responsibility to society as a whole—a responsibility to help shape our shared culture in a positive way and a responsibility to make their tools of communication widely available, in keeping with the idea of an open, accessible Internet. Like many of us, these media executives—publishers, producers, editors, website creators, and so on—are eager consumers of the products they help to create. Many were motivated to pursue media careers because they grew up as fans. They *love* books, movies, newspapers, magazines, TV shows, websites, and other media products, and they want to create (and enable others to create) content that they can be proud of, enriching the experiences of millions of people through media products that inform, entertain, challenge, and move us. This motivation exists alongside the desire to get rich and, in our experience, surprisingly often outweighs it.

So even though media companies are generally *not* legally restricted in the kinds of content they can disseminate—especially in the United States—most have no desire to publish offerings that degrade or despoil our shared culture or host content that discourages free discourse. And that includes hate speech. The people and groups who want to use the self-publishing tools of the Internet to spread hatred and violence are almost entirely at the fringes of society; the leaders of the companies that largely control the media pipelines are as repulsed by their twisted philosophies as any of us. In this regard, they want to be good corporate citizens. (It's no accident that Google has adopted, as its informal company slogan, "Don't be evil.")

It might seem, then, that the problem of hate speech is relatively easy to solve. All that's needed is for the major media companies to agree to cease providing a technological platform to purveyors of hate, and in a short while hate-filled messages would all but disappear from our collective consciousness.

Unfortunately, matters are not that simple. Let's consider some of the practical, philosophical, economic, and legal realities that make it difficult for even the most well-intentioned media companies to completely eliminate hate speech from their offerings. As we do throughout this book, we'll focus primarily on Internet-based businesses, since the challenges posed by hate speech in the online age are new and uniquely complex—which is why we hope to contribute to their solution.

HATE SPEECH ON THE INTERNET: A PROBLEM OF SCOPE

One possible avenue of action for limiting the impact of hate speech on the Internet is through technological means. After all, the Internet is an incredible technological marvel, automatically connecting billions of separate nodes in a robust global network that makes possible virtually instantaneous communication. If the amazing speed and power of digital technology makes the Internet possible, why can't that same technology be used to control or filter some of the most offensive and potentially dangerous content of the web?

It's a tempting vision. After all, a purely technological solution to hate speech could, in theory at least, be applied neutrally and instantly, without the intervention of any individual, organization, or government agency, producing neutral results that everyone would be bound to respect. But this vision, alas, is mostly illusory. One crucial reason is the sheer *vastness* of the world of Internet content and the ease with which anyone and everyone can contribute to it.

Statistics convey some sense of the challenge. As of mid-2012, an estimated 2.4 billion people around the world had become active users of the Internet. This includes hundreds of millions of users on every continent—not just 273 million people in North America (which you might expect) but over 167 million people in Africa and more than a billion in Asia. And since the Internet is above all an *interactive* medium,

these people are not just passive recipients of data but potential con-
tributors of content to the ever-rising tide of material that is available
to practically everyone, everywhere.[1]

As for the depth and scope of that tide, plumbing the vastness of
the Internet is almost as difficult as measuring the breadth of the universe, but by any measure it is unthinkably huge and expanding at a
breathtaking rate. One reasonable estimate suggests that as of November 2012, the number of webpages indexed on Google is at least 50
billion, up from a "mere" 20 billion just two years earlier.[2] By way of
comparison, if we equate one webpage with a single page in a book
(almost certainly an underestimate), that's the equivalent of some 167
million average-size books, or about five times the size of the Library
of Congress. So when we talk about "moderating," "editing," or "filtering" the Internet, we are talking about managing an almost incalculable
flood of content. Sorting the grains of sand on the beach by size, shape,
and color would be considerably easier.

In recent years, social media sites have become some of the most
popular launching pads for Internet exploration. As a result, the
number of users and the volume of content they produce and access
have grown exponentially. For example, as of October 2012, YouTube
claimed 280 million members who uploaded an average of seventy-
two hours of video content to the site *every minute of every day.* And as
we've already mentioned, Facebook recently surpassed the one billion
mark on its member rolls, making it the equivalent of the third-largest
nation in the world (after China and India).

For all these reasons, technological solutions to the problem of
hate speech are extremely limited. Years ago, ADL developed a software
tool called HateFilter, which was designed for parents to use in home
computers to filter out some of the most offensive hate sites. Primarily
intended for use as an educational tool, it blocked access to sites of hate
groups and redirected the user to information about hate groups at the

ADL home page. It was extremely difficult for the creators of HateFilter to stay abreast of the continually evolving world of hate speech. Today, in the infinitely more complex universe of social media and user-generated content, an effective filter is not conceivable.

The fact is that it is virtually impossible for any software program to keep up with all the possible, and continually proliferating, varieties of online hate. Like every other form of human communication, bigoted or hateful speech is always evolving, changing its vocabulary and style, adjusting to social and demographic trends, and reaching out in new ways to potentially receptive new audiences. Hatemongers, like other marketers, are constantly on the lookout for new targets, new themes, and new ways to package their message. Which means that, as soon as the monitors have deciphered and catalogued the current terms of abuse, conspiracy theories, vile accusations, and historical distortions favored by the hatemongers, a new crop has likely been developed.

As a small example, consider the vast, cryptic, and continually morphing set of visual and verbal symbols used by extremist organizations to convey their ideas to followers as well as to curious observers. Like corporate logos, these symbols express powerful ideas in a compact, compelling form—and like corporate logos, they are constantly being "tweaked" and innovated to keep up with the latest warped thinking of their users. That's why an entire subsection of ADL's website is dedicated to a continually updated analysis of symbols currently being used by extremist groups. The latest assortment includes graphic images (ranging from the obvious—the swastika and "iron cross" of the Nazis—to the arcane—a "spider web" tattoo that is apparently earned by racist prison inmates as a reward for killing a minority group member), as well as numerical symbols (88, 33/6, 4/19) and obscure acronyms (RAHOWA, WPWW, UAO) charged with secret, hateful meanings.[3]

It would take an incredibly sophisticated software program—constantly updated by a large staff of human researchers—to scan the contents of the Internet in search of such secret tools for transmitting messages of hate. And how could any technological system analyze the context in which these symbols appear to accurately separate hate-oriented usages from innocent ones? After all, the number 88 doesn't only represent the letters HH, as in "Heil Hitler!"—it also denotes the number of keys on a piano, the atomic number of the element radium, and, in ham radio lingo, the affectionate signoff "hugs and kisses." It's all too likely that most "hate-scanning" software systems would inaccurately flag millions of innocuous webpages as containing hate speech, potentially creating damage that would take countless hours of human effort to uncover and repair.

It's nice to imagine a purely technological solution to the challenge of tracking and marginalizing hate speech on the Internet. Alas, the reality of the problem makes it clear that, while technology can play a helpful role, it offers nothing remotely like a complete solution.

STOPPING POLLUTION NEAR THE SOURCE: THE ROLE OF INTERNET HOSTS

More effective and more important, we believe, are efforts that we at the ADL and other organizations have mounted to seek voluntary cooperation of the Internet community to join in a concerted, long-term campaign against hate speech. The first line of defense in this campaign is the companies that host the hate-filled content. (The largest hosts of Internet content these days are social media companies, like Facebook, YouTube, and Twitter, that provide self-publishing outlets for billions of people. Here, however, we are talking about companies that host websites, e-commerce sites, music distribution hubs, online gaming content, and so on.) Most of these host companies are invisible and largely unknown to the general public, although there are some well-known Internet brand names, like AOL, Yahoo!, and GoDaddy.

As in other areas related to hate speech, the role of law in controlling the behavior of Internet intermediaries is limited. In this case, a specific law mandates that limitation. Section 230 of the Communications Decency Act shields interactive computer services (including ISPs and websites) from liability by stating, "No provider or user of an interactive computer service shall be treated as the publisher or speaker of any information provided by another information content provider." Passed in response to some court decisions early in the Internet era that started to hold Internet hosts responsible for the content posted by users, this rule is intended to promote user content on the Internet and has become a major bulwark defending Internet companies from legal responsibility for the content they make available. Unlike the editor of a newspaper, the publisher of a book, or the director of a television network, the manager of an Internet intermediary is not expected to scrutinize and approve the content he or she makes available to the public. This sometimes results in the perverse situation of a newspaper, for example, being legally responsible for the content in its print edition while the Internet intermediary is immune from legal liability for the same content published in the paper's online edition.

Without the threat of legal liability to prompt Internet hosts to act on Internet hate, if they are to play a constructive role in reducing the volume of online hate, it will have to be through voluntary efforts, not by force of the law.

The first and perhaps most important step would be stricter enforcement of the terms of service included in user contracts, which empower Internet hosts to drop offensive content from the sites they serve. These terms of service generally include some limitation on the kind of content that will be hosted and made available on the Internet. For example, users are required to agree that they will not use the service to send spam or computer viruses through the Internet and that they will not violate the copyrights of others by reproducing protected content.

In addition, one typical agreement requires the user to agree that he or she will not:

> Post or transmit any unlawful, threatening, abusive, libelous, defamatory, obscene, pornographic, profane, or otherwise objectionable information of any kind, including without limitation any transmissions constituting or encouraging conduct that would constitute a criminal offense, give rise to civil liability, or otherwise violate any local, state, national or international law, including without limitation the U.S. export control laws and regulations.[4]

This particular set of rules doesn't specify "hate speech," but, as we've discussed, some forms of hate speech certainly qualify as "threatening, abusive, libelous, defamatory, [or] obscene." If more Internet hosts, especially in the United States, can be persuaded to take steps to block blatantly hate-filled content within the limits permitted by their terms of service, it will at least be more difficult for the most egregious hatemongers to gain access through respectable hosts.

Of course, Internet hosts make revenues and profits from the fees they charge for hosting websites. In financial terms, turning away customers gains them nothing other than the satisfaction their managers may feel from knowing they've played a responsible role as citizens of the Internet world. As a result, many of these companies are unlikely to make much of an effort to proactively seek out violations of their terms of service governing "threatening" or "abusive" content. The onus is on users of the Internet, including both concerned individuals and watchdog organizations like ADL, to call offensive content to the attention of the Internet hosts. Our experience suggests that at least some hosts are responsive to such complaints.

However, there are limits to the effectiveness of this strategy. There are many Internet hosts, the costs of becoming a host are low, and individuals or groups seeking access to the Internet as a way of spreading hatred will probably always be able to find a company willing to hold its nose and host their site in exchange for a fee. And as we saw in chapter one, there are even hate-oriented individuals, like "Farm Belt Fuehrer" Gary Lauck, who have established companies for the specific purpose of providing Internet access to other hatemongers. As long as the Internet hosting business remains highly decentralized and easy to join—and as long as bigotry continues to represent a profitable "niche" that unscrupulous business owners are willing to exploit—hosts won't represent a useful "chokepoint" in the effort to keep hatred from finding a home online.

PORTALS TO THE WEB: THE ROLE OF SEARCH ENGINES

During the 1990s and 2000s, as the Internet evolved, expanded, and became enormously more complex, users needed more and more technological help to locate content that interested them. Enter the search engine—a powerful, highly sophisticated form of software capable of scanning hundreds of millions of webpages within a second or two in search of particular kinds of data, language, or imagery and then sorting the results in a fashion that users find helpful and informative. Most of us who have come to rely on the Internet as our chief daily source of ideas, news, and entertainment can scarcely imagine how we would track down the content we like without the services of a great search engine. And of course the company that dominates this incredibly important and lucrative corner of the Internet universe is Google, with an estimated sixty-seven percent of the U.S. search engine market.[5] Companies like Microsoft, with its Bing search engine, are challenging Google's dominance with new forms of search engines and different user experiences.

In a world where search engines are primary portals for Internet users, cooperation from the Googles of the world is another important goal for those of us who are determined to combat the spread of hate speech. We understand that search engine operators seek to apply search algorithm technology with little human intervention as to the results a user sees; their job is to display what is on the Internet. But we also understand that computer-generated search results can give prominence to hate sites, resulting in misleading search results for those seeking truthful and accurate information and providing undue publicity to content that previously languished in well-deserved obscurity. The role of search engine operators in fighting online hate remains fraught with complicated challenges.

As we've noted, companies like Google have neither the resources nor the will necessary to act as "private censors" of the Internet. Even if Google wanted to examine every new webpage before clearing it to appear in response to a search query, the company would probably need a staff of hundreds of thousands to handle the task. Technology is not really up to the task of making judgments about whether content qualifies as hate speech.

Furthermore, such an approach, even if it were practicable, would require an endless variety of complex judgment calls. The results would be certain to antagonize almost as many people as they would gratify. They'd also likely subject Google to unending public criticisms and political attacks for censorship.

Given these realities, it's understandable that companies like Google choose instead to tackle the problem of dishonest, dangerous, or vicious Internet content—including hate speech—on a case-by-case basis, responding largely to complaints raised by outside individuals, organizations, and sometimes governments. This places much of the burden on watchdog organizations like ADL. We seek to work cooperatively with

Google to address hate speech while avoiding interference with the ag-nostic search result philosophy of the company.

Consider, for example, the story of the notoriously anti-Semitic website Jew Watch. In a sense, the creators of this site deserve points for honesty. They make no bones about the bigoted nature of the content they present. High on the site's home page is this description of its purpose:

The Jew Watch Project Is The Internet's Largest Scholarly Collection of Articles on Zionist History_Free Educational Library for Private Study, Scholarship, Research & News About Zionism_We Reveal Zionist Bank-sters, News Falsifiers, PR Liars, Neocons, Subversives, Terrorists & Spies_ The Jew Watch Project's 1.5 Billion Pages Served Demonstrate Our Focus on Professionalism._An Oasis of News for Americans Who Presently En-dure the Hateful Censorship of Zionist Occupation.[6]

The rest of the site lives up to this billing. Jew Watch is an ency-clopedic compilation of virtually every anti-Semitic myth, stereotype, and conspiracy theory known to humankind, treating Jews not just as virtually equivalent to "Communists" but as the source of almost ev-ery imaginable evil in human history. Not only does Jew Watch deny the existence of the Holocaust, but it turns the tables on conventional history by providing a lengthy list of alleged "Jewish Genocides Today and Yesterday" (that is, genocides supposedly organized by powerful Jewish masterminds). Its list of "Jewish Leaders, Conspirators, Power Lords" includes every name you might expect and quite a few almost no reasonable person would expect (Dwight D. Eisenhower? Winston Churchill? Nancy Pelosi?). In short, Jew Watch is the product of a col-lection of seemingly paranoid minds who view world history through an amazingly distorted lens and see virtually everything as a confirma-tion of the vicious, sub-human nature of Jews and Judaism.

If Jew Watch does not epitomize "hate speech," then nothing does. It would be tempting and easy to ignore this collection of semi-sane ravings—were it not for the fact that any routine Google search for the word "Jew" accords Jew Watch a prominent place in the rankings. (When we recently conducted such a search, Jew Watch popped up fifth on the list.) And unfortunately, countless users of the Internet (especially those who are young and naive) assume that a high ranking in a Google search is a virtual endorsement of the site's content—that the ranking is a mark of reliability, credibility, and authoritativeness.

The high ranking of Jew Watch in response to routine search inquiries was not due to a conscious choice by Google, but was solely a result of the company's automated system of page ranking. This system—based on an enormously complex set of algorithms that are continually being "tweaked" and refined—ranks the importance and relevance of webpages based not on the subjective judgments of any individual but on objective, instantaneously measurable criteria such as the number of external links a particular URL has received. The theory is that a page that has been linked to by a larger number of outside pages has been judged to be relevant and interesting by a significant number of web users, and therefore may be worthy of attention by web surfers investigating a particular topic.

In many cases, Google's algorithms work astonishingly well, producing a list of relevant, timely, and useful links on a particular topic drawn from hundreds of thousands of millions of possibilities within fractions of a second. But no system is flawless, and that includes Google's search engine. It is said that Google page rankings are subject to deliberate manipulation by web designers who have experimented with the algorithm and figured out ways to elevate the rankings of particular pages in defiance of what "common sense" or ordinary good judgment might dictate. In relatively benign form, this process is often called "search engine optimization." It's used by webpage designers and marketers to enhance the visibility of contents on the Internet, promote companies and products, and attract more visitors to particular sites. In a less-honest, sometimes sinister form, it's known as "Google bombing"—the deliberate creation of thousands of phony web links in order to elevate a particular page to the top of the search engine rankings despite the lack of any logical or authentic relevance for its contents.

Sometimes Google bombing is done with political or satiric purposes. For example, political opponents of President George W. Bush used Google bombing to ensure that the phrase "miserable failure" would automatically generate links to pages about Bush. (Unwilling to allow its search engine results to be manipulated for such purposes— and fearful that users would assume that Google was the source of the obvious political bias these rankings embodied—the company reportedly altered its algorithms to ensure that searches for "miserable failure" now generate primarily links to sites that discuss the tactic of Google bombing itself.)

But more subtle forms of Google bombing are said to be used by savvy webpage designers to distort search engine rankings on behalf of basically valueless webpages. Such is likely the case with Jew Watch.

When ADL met with the leaders of Google to point out the prominent ranking of Jew Watch, the offensive nature of the website, and the frankly misleading nature of the search results, Google took action. It placed text on its site that apologized for the ranking and gave users a clear explanation of how search results are obtained, to refute the impression that Jew Watch was somehow being validated as a reliable source of information.

To this day, if you search the word "Jew" on Google, the first handful of results will include the following message from the search engine itself:

An explanation of our search results

If you recently used Google to search for the word "Jew," you may have seen results that were very disturbing. We assure you that the views expressed by the sites in your results are not in any way endorsed by Google. We'd like to explain why you're seeing these results when you conduct this search.

A site's ranking in Google's search results is automatically determined by computer algorithms using thousands of factors to calculate a page's relevance to a given query. Sometimes subtleties of language cause anomalies to appear that cannot be predicted. A search for "Jew" brings up one such unexpected result.

If you use Google to search for "Judaism," "Jewish" or "Jewish people," the results are informative and relevant. So why is a search for "Jew" different? One reason is that the word "Jew" is often used in an anti-Semitic context. Jewish organizations are more likely to use the word "Jewish" when talking about members of their faith. The word has become somewhat charged linguistically, as noted on websites devoted to Jewish topics such as these:

http://shakti.trincoll.edu/~mendele/vol01/vol01.174

http://www.jewishworldreview.com/cols/jonah081500.asp

Someone searching for information on Jewish people would be more likely to enter terms like "Judaism," "Jewish people," or "Jews" than the single word "Jew." In fact, prior to this incident, the word "Jew" only appeared about once in every 10 million search queries. Now it's likely that the great majority of searches on Google for "Jew" are by people who have heard about this issue and want to see the results for themselves.

Our search results are generated completely objectively and are independent of the beliefs and preferences of those who work at Google.

Some people concerned about this issue have created online petitions to encourage us to remove particular links or otherwise adjust search results. Because of our objective and automated ranking system, Google cannot be influenced by these petitions. The only sites we omit are those we are legally compelled to remove or those maliciously attempting to manipulate our results.

We apologize for the upsetting nature of the experience you had using Google and appreciate your taking the time to inform us about it.

Sincerely, The Google Team

P.S. You may be interested in some additional information the Anti-Defamation League has posted about this issue at http://www.adl.org/rumors/google_search_rumors.asp. In addition, we call your attention to both the Jewish Internet Association, an organization that addresses online anti-semitism, at http://www.jewishinternetassociation.org/, and Google's search results on this topic.[7]

As we've already noted, we're strong advocates of counter-speech as a powerful tool for combating hate speech—in many ways, a far stronger tool than censorship or suppression. We think Google's effort to enlighten and inform its users about the implications of the word "Jew" in a society where anti-Semitism is a continuing problem represents counter-speech at its best: unbiased, fact-based, and available on the same basis and in the same location as the hateful speech to which it responds.

The Jew Watch case isn't the only instance in which we've worked behind the scenes with search engine companies to make their services more user friendly and less accommodating to hatemongers. For example, Google refuses to sell hate speech terms as "keywords" for advertising purposes, nor does it permit paid "sponsored links" to hate sites.

Cases like that of Jew Watch might suggest that one possible solution to the problem of online hate speech is through cooperation with companies like Google. Perhaps the day will come when hateful and deceitful rhetoric on the Internet automatically triggers a prompt, effective rebuttal. It would indeed be desirable for Google to ensure that other hate sites receive similar treatment to the one developed for Jew Watch. But there are a number of reasons that this can't be regarded as *the* solution to the challenge of online hate.

One reason that we've already cited is the sheer vastness of the challenge. The number of webpages is so huge and constantly expanding that it's fundamentally impossible for any company, no matter how well funded and well intentioned, to pro-actively monitor and evaluate every site for potentially abusive content.

Another reason is the continually evolving and morphing nature of online hate. It would be easy enough to create a mechanical system to locate specific offensive terms ("nigger," "kike," "faggot") and flag webpages that use them. But such a system runs the risk of unfairly targeting some sites whose purposes or contents are actually benign—an English teacher's analysis of Mark Twain's use of the word "nigger" in *Huckleberry Finn,* for example, or a historian's study of racist propaganda under the Third Reich—while overlooking less easily identified forms of bigotry such as Holocaust denial.

And simply dumping the problem in the lap of Google would put the company in a fundamentally untenable situation, asking it to adjudicate controversies that no private organization is really capable of impartially judging. As the thoughtful scholar Adam Thierer wrote in a *Forbes* column on the issue:

> [I]n theory, Google could "come up with a database of disputed claims" or "exercise a heavier curatorial control in presenting search results," as [essayist Evgency] Morozov advocates. But how desirable would it be

to have Google arbitrate every controversial claim under the sun? After all, one person's "heavier curatorial control" is another's censorship. It would also open Google up to charges of violating "search neutrality" principles and other antitrust-related claims.[8]

Google and other online search companies do indeed have a significant role to play in helping to combat the spread of viral hatred online. But unfortunately there's no simple solution to be created through an improved page ranking algorithm, a system of automatic links for disputed content, or some kind of "truth" or "civility test" administered by the search engine firms. The challenge of finding and responding to online hate will continue to demand vigilance and cooperative efforts by a number of parties, including companies like Google, monitoring groups like ADL, and concerned citizens themselves.

ONLINE COMMUNITIES: THE WORLDS OF SOCIAL MEDIA

As the Internet has evolved beyond the Web 1.0 world of websites and search engines to the Web 2.0 world of social media, the intermediaries with a vitally important role—perhaps the most important role—are the big social media companies, including Facebook, YouTube, and Twitter. For billions of people around the world, these have become primary portals into the online world—which means that user-generated hate speech, incendiary images, and other offensive content available through these media can spread with astonishing speed into countless homes.

Many assume that social media companies are open portals that exercise no control over the content of their pages. This impression is strengthened by the ease with which individuals can add content at will—writings, pictures, music, videos, links to outside sources, and much more. Members are free to create groups, connect to other individuals, and promote causes, products, or activities they like. A social media site like Facebook appears to be no more than a blank slate, like an empty bulletin board in a public park on which anyone can post any sort of notice with no prior control or editorial oversight.

All of this is true—to a point. But in fact the popular social media sites are businesses that have the power, the right, and (most would say) the obligation to exercise a degree of control over how their pages are used. They are more like the community bulletin board you might find in the entrance way of your local supermarket, where the store manager retains the ability to scan posted notices and remove those he deems unsuitable.

One way the sites exercise their right of control is by limiting access. Facebook, for example, theoretically restricts access to those over age thirteen—but many younger kids are known to find a way to participate, with or without their parents' permission.

Another way is by limiting the kinds of content people can post. Take YouTube, for example. Although the number and variety of video content it contains are mind-bogglingly vast, it is not unlimited. One reason is that copyright law imposes liability on YouTube for the posting of illegal content by its users, unless the company takes certain steps to prevent it or take it down. YouTube makes enormous efforts to make sure that movies and TV shows are not available without the permission of the copyright holder. And YouTube goes to great lengths to ensure that pornography is not broadcast through its service. A clever automatic algorithm, for example, is used to detect and eliminate pornography even before anyone spots it and complains about it.

YouTube also has a list of other specific types of content it tries to ban. The list, as posted on YouTube's community guidelines page, includes "bad stuff like animal abuse, drug abuse, under-age drinking and smoking, or bomb making," "[g]raphic or gratuitous violence," "gross-out videos of accidents, dead bodies, or similar things intended to shock or disgust," and "predatory behavior, stalking, threats, harassment, intimidation, invading privacy, revealing other people's personal information, and inciting others to commit violent acts."

Most relevant to our theme, users are warned to avoid "hate speech (speech which attacks or demeans a group based on race or ethnic origin, religion, disability, gender, age, veteran status, and sexual orientation/gender identity)."[9] Helpful examples of each of these categories of barred content are provided on the site. Nonetheless, these guidelines undoubtedly have a subjective element, which means they would be exceedingly difficult or impossible to enforce through the use of technological systems or content-analysis algorithms. Actively engaged human intelligence must be employed in the process.

Other social networks have created similar guidelines. Facebook, for example, has a set of community standards that includes this statement: "Facebook does not permit hate speech. While we encourage you to challenge ideas, institutions, events, and practices, it is a serious violation to attack a person based on their race, ethnicity, national origin, religion, sex, gender, sexual orientation, disability or medical condition."

Guidelines like these are important and valuable, as far as they go. One of the big problems, of course, is how to enforce them. Here the problem of scope rears its head. The huge numbers of members that popular social media sites boast and the vast volume of content these members post make it impossible for the staffs of the host companies to pro-actively monitor and edit the contents. As we've seen, the only way content guidelines—in particular, those related to hate speech—can be applied is through the active engagement of real people examining the content and using their judgment as to whether it is acceptable.

Almost inevitably, this task falls mainly on the users of the social media sites. Each company has its own system for soliciting and channeling user input. Registered YouTube members, for example, can click a button to "flag" a video for review by their company's content-analysis team. The company claims that most flagged videos are reviewed and acted on within an hour of posting.

At ADL, we do our best to monitor the ever-changing worlds of social media and to communicate with the company experts whose job it is to police the online content. Having worked with Facebook and Google in particular, we can report that these companies take online hate seriously. They have dedicated staffs and work hard to keep up with the tidal wave of online hate. They'd like to keep their sites safe and civil and avoid being associated with bigotry and hatred.

In May 2012, Facebook hosted a program at its headquarters in Menlo Park, CA, for Internet experts and members of the ADL community in the Bay area. It was moving to hear from a senior Facebook executive whose parents were Holocaust survivors about the searing personal impact of online hate. Likewise, a Facebook manager responsible for responding to complaints about online content spoke eloquently at an ADL event in Houston in the fall of 2012 about his staff's real concern over the impact that hate speech can have on people. Facebook "gets it": Its leaders understand that the social network can be a platform for free expression and worldwide communication that connects people and promotes democracy as well as a platform that respects personal dignity and promotes civility by restricting online hate.

Google also has stepped up to the plate. The cooperation in the "Jew Watch" episode was noted previously. Executives at its YouTube unit also have engaged significantly with ADL, appearing at a recent program in the New York Times Center in New York and hosting a multi-stakeholder meeting on Internet hate at Google's Mountain View, CA, campus.

Yet challenges remain. Even with the real cooperation of social media companies on the problem of Internet hate, staffs are limited and the flow of new content is vast. It's simply impossible for a company like Facebook to pro-actively monitor the pictures, links, and writings that members post online; employees have their hands full responding to the thousands of complaints they must field every week concerning content that someone finds offensive.

In many cases, we think the social media companies do a reasonably good job of managing the sometimes tricky decisions about what constitutes hate speech as opposed to material that is simply "edgy" or "controversial" and should not be curbed. In other cases, we are not hesitant to call them out. For example, Facebook does not regard Holocaust denial as hate speech—a judgment with which we disagree.

Some applications of Facebook's community standards produce results that seem skewed. Consider, for example, the user-generated Facebook page titled "Jewish Memes" (http://www.facebook.com/jewishmemes). Interspersed among a collection of juvenile but harmless jokes involving Jewish people and themes are a number of unquestionably anti-Semitic assaults—for instance, a photo of Holocaust victim Anne Frank with the caption, "What's that burning? Oh it's my family"—as well as countless "gags" turning on traditional anti-Semitic stereotype (Jews as misers, Jews as loan sharks, etc.). The page bears a bracketed subtitle required by Facebook personnel, "[Controversial Humor]," but with this user-generated disclaimer:

Welcome to Jewish Memes! 100% Memes, 100% Kosher. NOTICE: The "Controversial Humor" tag has been added by the facebook administration by a huge misunderstanding. There is nothing offensive about that page. If you think that it is unjustified, contact fb.

As you can imagine, Facebook has received many complaints about Jewish Memes. When Australian Race Relations Commissioner Dr. Helen Szoke declared that the page might violate local hate speech laws, access to it from computer servers based in Australia was restricted. But a Facebook spokesman has defended the continuing availability of the page from other venues, saying, "Hate speech against protected categories is against Facebook's terms. However, humorous content is still allowed to target those categories. Ultimately, this is an issue of free speech—these pages are clearly offensive to some but as they are not targeting individuals, are based on humor and make no credible threat of violence they will not be removed."[10]

Opinions on specific cases like this one will vary. In our judgment, the "humor" defense creates a loophole big enough to permit a vast amount of incredibly hateful content to permeate Facebook under a thin veil of acceptability. A Woody Allen routine poking fun at his own Jewish upbringing is one thing, a cartoon that purports to find comedy in the gas ovens at Auschwitz is quite another. We don't think it's terribly difficult to see the difference. And a halfway solution like mandating the use of the label "[Controversial Humor]" is less than satisfactory; indeed, like labeling contents "Adults Only" while creating no actual restrictions on access, it may simply invite additional attention to a site by those who are actively seeking out the titillation that tasteless pseudo-humor can provide.

An even more egregious example—one that, thankfully, was ultimately resolved appropriately—involved a Facebook page dedicated to what it called "The Third Palestinian Intifada." For those who may not know, the first and second intifada were armed Palestinian uprisings (taking place in 1987–1991 and 2000–2004, respectively) in which some 1,500 Israeli citizens were killed in acts of terror, including suicide bombings and drive-by shootings. The page dedicated to promoting a third such uprising, posted on Facebook beginning early in 2011, called openly for the destruction of Israel. As translated by experts at SITE Monitoring Service, an organization dedicated to studying the international terrorist threat, the page read, in part:

The march to Palestine [referring, in this case, to the land generally known as Israel] will start in the neighboring countries of Palestine on May 15th. After our recent recognition we will be marching throughout all Islamic countries and Palestine will be liberated and free. Our goal is to reach millions of subscribers on this page before May. Rise up, publish this page everywhere, we are coming O Palestine. . . . Copy the link, put it in your profile, and publish it with your pictures and videos and with all pages everywhere. . . . The Palestinian cause is our cause. Publish this page on the sites, forums and elsewhere and invite all your friends to participate. If everyone is invited, all friends and Allah's will, we will reach more than 100,000 members a day.[11]

Despite protests from the government of Israel, ADL, other Jewish community groups, and countless individuals, the page remained up, defended by Facebook spokespeople as an appropriate expression of "political ideology." The hoped-for numbers proved highly conservative. By March, the page had more than 350,000 "likes" and was growing at a rate of 25,000 per day. And as the popularity of the page grew, so did the concerns of its opponents (who of course launched counterspeech Facebook pages of their own).

Finally, the controversy crossed a tipping point. On March 29, 2011, Facebook yielded to the majority of its users and removed the Third Intifada page. The company's explanation stated, in part:

The page . . . began as a call for peaceful protest, even though it used a term that has been associated with violence in the past. In addition, the administrators initially removed comments that promoted violence. However, after the publicity of the page, more comments deteriorated to direct calls for violence. Eventually, the administrators also participated in these calls. After administrators of the page received repeated warnings about posts that violated our policies, we removed the page.

We continue to believe that people on Facebook should be able to express their opinions, and we don't typically take down content that speaks out against countries, religions, political entities, or ideas. However, we monitor pages that are reported to us and when they degrade to direct calls for violence or expressions of hate—as occurred in this case—we have and will continue to take them down.[12]

We were pleased by the final disposition of the Third Intifada case, though disappointed that it took so long for Facebook to reach what seemed to us the obvious decision. In similar fashion, it took a long campaign by ADL and other groups to persuade Facebook to delete pages maintained by Hezbollah, despite its designation by the U.S. State Department as a foreign terrorist organization ineligible to receive "material support or resources" from American citizens or entities. Twitter and YouTube, however, continue to provide access to Hezbollah, a policy position we deplore as short-sighted and misguided. Indeed, in the Gaza crisis of fall 2012, Twitter hosted materials purporting to come from Hamas.

One of our responsibilities at ADL is to monitor decisions made by major gatekeepers like Facebook, YouTube, and Twitter and draw independent conclusions about their appropriateness. And so, at the same time that we will work cooperatively behind the scenes to advise various social media companies about trends and issues we think they need to follow and address, we will criticize them publicly and attempt to pressure them when we believe they are making a mistake.

The Internet continues to evolve. New content continually is emerging, creating new kinds of connections that raise fresh questions. For example, the online merchant Amazon has arguably become a major curator of cultural content through its sales of books, music, movies, and other media products. ADL has worked with Amazon and other online merchants to help them develop sound policies for dealing with offensive materials. For example, while both Amazon and Barnes & Noble continue to sell offensive books online, the pages describing anti-Semitic works, such as the *Protocols of the Elders of Zion,* come with a note from the ADL explaining why these books are dishonest and offensive.

THE QUESTION OF ANONYMITY

You know that an issue has entered the mainstream when it's the subject of an episode of a major television series. It happened with the issue of Internet anonymity in 2012 when Aaron Sorkin's topical series *The Newsroom* tackled the problem head-on.

As you may know, the series stars Jeff Daniels in the role of Will McAvoy, the anchor and managing editor of a fictitious show called *News Night.* In episode six, "Bullies," McAvoy is disgusted by the inanity of the user comments from the show's website—posted by anonymous viewers with handles like "LollypopLollypop" and "SurrenderDorothee"— that he is required to read on the air. When the show ends, he storms off the set and confronts Dev Patel in the role of Neal Sampat, the young producer who is in charge of managing the site (we've streamlined the dialogue slightly by skipping a couple of Sorkin's trademark wisecracks):

> MCAVOY: Is there any way of knowing if LollypopLollypop is ten years
>   old? Or a basset hound?
>
> SAMPAT: No. . . .
>
> MCAVOY: Is there any way of knowing if LollypopLollypop and
>   SurrenderDorothee are the same person?
>
> SAMPAT: No. . . .
>
> MCAVOY: Here's what I'd love. You want to join the discussion? Fine.
>   I want to know your name, age, occupation, and level of
>   education.

> SAMPAT (protesting): The thing about the Internet is, it's a populist
>   tool.
>
> MCAVOY: Populists have names too—William Jennings Bryan, Will
>   Rogers, me. Unless you're Deep Throat or in the witness
>   protection program, anonymity is cowardice. You're in a mob,
>   you're lobbing smack from the cheap seats. . . .

McAvoy decrees that, henceforth, no one will be allowed to post a comment on the *News Night* website without revealing his or her true identity. Emily Mortimer, playing the producer "Mac" McHale, tries to intervene:

> MCHALE: Won't the result be that nobody posts comments on our
>   website anymore?
>
> MCAVOY: (sarcastically) First of all, oh no! What will we do without
>   feedback from SurrenderDorothee!? And second, the result will
>   be that our website will ghettoize every other website! The result
>   will be civility in the public square and a triumph of populism!
>   I'm going to single-handedly fix the Internet!

Unfortunately for Will McAvoy, not only does the rule change not instantaneously fix the Internet, but its chief result is to prompt a death threat aimed at McAvoy himself. That's Hollywood for you.

Hollywood or no, Sorkin may be on to something. We believe that one useful step in encouraging greater tolerance online—and discouraging hate speech—may be to challenge the custom of anonymity.

Facebook has over a billion users who are required to use their real names. Facebook's "Name Policy" page reads, in part, "Facebook is a community where people use their real identities. We require everyone to provide their real names, so you always know who you're connecting with. . . . The name you use should be your real name as it would be listed on your credit card, student ID, etc.[13] As with any regulation, individuals try to skirt the rule; Facebook has estimated that about 8.7 percent of its pages use names that are "duplicates, mis-classified, or undesirable."[14] In the vast Facebook universe, that means tens of millions of less-than-transparent page names—but a 92.3 percent compliance rate strikes us as impressive. It means that the vast majority of Facebook users are identified with and accountable for the contents they post.

It is time for more companies to consider adopting Facebook's real-name policy, with the recognition that the value of anonymity for free-expression purposes and to protect privacy may sometimes outweigh the real-name requirements. People who are able to post anonymously (or pseudonymously) are far more likely to say awful things, sometimes with awful effects. Speaking from behind a blank wall that shields a person from responsibility encourages recklessness—it's far easier to simply hit the "send" button without a second thought under those circumstances.

Other effects of anonymity on behavior may be more subtle. Shortly after editor Michael Marshall was asked to take over the chore of moderating online comments at the magazine *New Scientist*, he was moved to write a column speculating about the psychological mechanisms behind the startling abuse even innocuous articles often attracted:

> Social psychologists have known for decades that, if we reduce our sense
> of our own identity—a process called deindividuation—we are less likely
> to stick to social norms. For example, in the 1960s Leon Mann studied a
> nasty phenomenon called "suicide baiting"—when someone threatening
> to jump from a high building is encouraged to do so by bystanders. Mann
> found that people were more likely to do this if they were part of a large
> crowd, if the jumper was above the 7th floor, and if it was dark. These
> are all factors that allowed the observers to lose their own individuality.

Social psychologist Nicholas Epley argues that much the same thing happens with online communication such as email. Psychologically, we are "distant" from the person we're talking to and less focused on our own identity. As a result we're more prone to aggressive behaviour, he says.[15]

If "deindividuation" encourages aggression even in a simple email, how much worse might the effect be in a completely anonymous comment page or website, particularly when emotionally charged political, religious, and social controversies are involved? The resulting abuse extends to hate-filled and inflammatory comments appended to the online versions of newspaper articles—comments that hijack legitimate discussions of current events and discourage thoughtful people from participating. Anonymity also facilitates the posting of anti-Semitic, racist, and homophobic content across the web, as well as the use of the Internet for cyber-bullying and other kinds of personal attacks. (For more on the problem of cyber-bullying, including some information on what schools and communities can do to combat it, see Appendixes D and E.)

To be sure, there is value in someone being able to use the Internet without being identified. Online privacy is a major issue today. Users of the Internet shouldn't have to feel that they sacrifice their right to privacy simply by virtue of posting a comment on a website or a social network page. And in the United States, we have had a great tradition of anonymous political speech, tracing back to such seminal documents as the *Federalist Papers* (originally published under the pseudonym "Publius"). Elsewhere, dissidents in oppressive regimes have felt free to speak up precisely because they believe (perhaps erroneously) that they cannot be identified.

Organizations like the Electronic Frontier Foundation have staunchly defended anonymity partly because of the protection it can provide to those whose right to dissent might otherwise be crushed. They cite cases like that of Wael Ghonim, an Egyptian activist who created an anonymous Facebook page called "We Are All Khaled Said," in honor of a human rights supporter martyred by police. Ghonim's page was shut down in November 2010 by Facebook administrators until a compromise was reached that allowed the page to be hosted by a sympathetic third party. The page eventually played a role in helping to recruit young Egyptians to join the Arab Spring movement.

Advocates of free expression point to cases like these to defend some uses of anonymity online. Joichi Ito, head of the Media Lab at the Massachusetts Institute of Technology, puts it this way: "The real risk to the world is if information technology pivots to a completely authentic identity for everyone. In the U.S., maybe you don't mind. If every kid in Syria, every time they used the Internet, their identity was visible, they would be dead."[16]

Thus, it's clear that there are some specific circumstances in which anonymity can play a positive social role. (For a stimulating sample of arguments for and against anonymity on the Internet, see the collection of letters about the topic in Appendix C.) But we need to ask whether these benefits of anonymity are being purchased at too high a price.

Internet intermediaries are wrestling with this issue. Google's fledgling social network, Google+, initially joined Facebook in requiring members to use their own real names. Later, amid criticism and controversy, Google+ reversed this decision. In July 2012, YouTube (which is owned by Google) announced a new policy designed to discourage anonymity: when someone comments on a video or uploads a new one, he or she is prompted to display a full name and to link to a Google profile, if any. Those who refuse this request are asked to provide a reason. And in January 2013, a French court ordered Twitter to identify users who posted messages that violated French laws against racism and anti-Semitism.

There are middle-ground positions possible: for example, permitting anonymity in specific circumstances or discouraging anonymity yet permitting it. The *New York Times* now has a policy of printing comments by registered users first, thereby giving them "premium placement" in the online community.

In the free-for-all that is American democracy, it's common for virtually every issue to find its way into the halls of the state and national legislatures. Online anonymity is no exception. Attempts have been made—for example, through a bill proposed in the New York State Senate in 2012—to limit anonymous postings. (The bill in question would require website administrators to delete comments on request unless attached to real names.) Nonetheless, in our view, this notion of promulgating a new standard of accountability online is not a matter for government intervention, given the strictures of the First Amendment.

A fascinating and instructive comparison can be drawn between the issue of online anonymity and that of wearing masks in public—a practice that can also be both benign (as in a Halloween or Mardi Gras parade) or threatening (as when members of the Ku Klux Klan cover their faces during cross-burning ceremonies).

More than eighteen states and localities have over the years passed "anti-masking" laws that make it a crime to wear a mask in public, particularly with intent to threaten or intimidate. Most of the laws were passed in response to the activities of the Ku Klux Klan, and they have generally passed constitutional muster because they have been deemed reasonable efforts to deter violence rather than attempts to suppress the symbolic expression of viewpoints.

Nonetheless, First Amendment issues are at stake with anti-masking statutes beyond the expressive speech issues. In a series of cases, the Supreme Court has made it clear that citizens have the right to communicate and associate anonymously, without fear of harassment or reprisals by others who oppose their views.

For example, the 1958 Supreme Court case *NAACP v. Alabama* made it clear that the government cannot require groups to reveal members' names and addresses unless public officials have a compelling need for the information and no alternative means of obtaining it.[17] And in the 1995 case *McIntyre v. Ohio Elections Commission*, the court struck down an ordinance prohibiting the anonymous distribution of political leaflets, saying, "Anonymity is a shield from the tyranny of the majority. It thus exemplifies the purpose behind the Bill of Rights, and of the First Amendment in particular: to protect unpopular individuals from retaliation—and their ideas from suppression—at the hand of an intolerant society."[18]

Some have suggested the KKK anti-masking laws might serve as models for a law requiring online identification of those who engage in hate speech. For example, in 2008, a Kentucky legislator proposed a ban on the posting of anonymous messages online. The proposed law would have required users to register their true names and addresses before contributing to any discussion forum. The stated goal was the elimination of "online bullying."

There were a host of problems with the proposed Kentucky law, which presumably is why it made little progress in the legislature. Similar proposals requiring online identification would face similar hurdles.

First, a broad prohibition on anonymous speech (which is essentially what the law would create) surely would run afoul of the Supreme Court's views on the right to remain anonymous as set forth in *McIntyre*. Second, the requirement that real names be used implicates *NAACP v. Alabama* as it would effectively be state law–ordered identification of a person's views and affiliations. Third, any attempt to define a more limited category of speech for which personal identification and accountability is required would face First Amendment problems. Most hate speech, no matter how objectionable, is permitted under the First Amendment, and defining what is in or out of bounds is nearly impossible in the abstract. Third, enforcement in this technological work-around age likely would be futile. Finally, the same laws designed to deter online defamation and harassment can also be used to target political dissent or silence whistleblowers for whom the option of remaining anonymous is critical. China requires real-name registration for a range of online activity precisely because of its chilling effects.

For all these reasons, the KKK anti-masking laws must be viewed as *sui generis,* not easily imported online.

So we're forced to conclude that law is not a remedy to the problems of online anonymity. But the legal restrictions that limit government action don't preclude action by private businesses like Facebook, Google, and the rest. It is time for Internet intermediaries voluntarily to consider requiring either the use of real names or the registration of real names in circumstances, such as the comments section for news articles, where the benefits of anonymous posting are outweighed by the need for greater online civility.

There is no bright-line test to define the proper circumstances, and undoubtedly Internet companies will need to experiment with a variety of policies over time to determine which systems work best and how the ideal of open but respectful discourse can be most effectively achieved. In any case, however, Internet sites permitting user-generated postings can and should make the judgment that in some instances the use of real names benefits society. We think that, in the long run, freedom of expression on the Internet will gain from a policy that asks individuals to take responsibility for the contents they post.

POLICING THE WEB—A COLLABORATIVE EFFORT

One of the themes of this book has been the enormous practical, social, political, and philosophical difficulties in developing fair, unbiased, enforceable, and generally acceptable methods for dealing with hate speech online. As we've seen, even defining hate speech can be profoundly complicated. For this reason, decisions concerning the regulation of online content that are made by one or a few people, behind closed doors, and announced as fiats by corporate or government officials are likely to be controversial, widely rejected, and ultimately unsustainable. The only practical solution, we believe, is a collaborative approach—one that brings a wide array of stakeholders to the table to discuss the challenges and opportunities openly and to strive to craft solutions that everyone can live with.

Now Facebook, Google, YouTube, and other leading services have a way to share best practices and to have ongoing discussions with groups like the ADL on what constitutes hate speech and what can be done about it.

In 2012, ADL helped to convene a new working group on online hate that is bringing together Internet industry leaders and others to probe the roots of the problem and develop new solutions to address it head-on. The Task Force on Internet Hate, created by the Inter-parliamentary Coalition for Combating Antisemitism (ICCA), formally approved a resolution in May establishing the Anti-Cyberhate Working Group, during their meeting under the auspices of the Stanford Center for Internet and Society in Palo Alto, CA. Our hope is that working alongside the Internet's leaders will allow for the development of industry standards that balance effectiveness with respect for the right to free speech.

The Anti-Cyberhate Working Group includes industry representatives, academics, nongovernmental organizations (NGOs), and others who are joining forces to "build best practices for understanding, reporting upon and responding to Internet hate." The new group represents an unprecedented opportunity for a collaborative approach to Internet hate.

There will be disagreements within the group, to be sure. There will be times when the online companies decide to allow certain content that others in the group consider hate speech prohibited by terms of service. Now, at least, there will be a regular place to have discussions, and there will be greater transparency about decision making.

Some people opposed to Internet hate think a better approach is for NGOs like ADL to have an adversarial relationship with Internet platforms, the better to publicly condemn mistaken decisions about Internet hate. Obviously, we disagree. The new group does not foreclose public criticism, and ADL will continue to be outspoken when necessary. But it does permit closer communication and opportunities for persuasion. Our strong belief is that it's preferable to have a seat at the table rather than remain outside in the hall when decisions are made about online hate.

We're convinced that if much of the time and energy spent advocating legal action against hate speech was used in collaborating and uniting with the online industry to fight the scourge of online hate, we would be making more gains in the fight.

The Anti-Cyberhate Working Group is still in its early stages. It will take time for us to develop overall policies that we think will help resolve some of the hate speech problems that plague the Internet. However, our preliminary conversations have suggested some broad areas of agreement:

- Intermediary companies (from ISPs and "online communities" to social media sites) should create clear hate speech policies and include them in the terms of service.
- Intermediaries should create mechanisms for enforcing hate speech policies in ways that preserve free speech and innovation.
- Intermediaries should make it easy for users to identify and report hate speech and to learn about the results of their inquiries.

- Intermediaries should strive for transparency about their hate speech reporting procedures, policies, and outcomes. This could include publishing some decisions about specific cases with explanations for the decisions made as a way of fostering dialogue, learning, and understanding as well as establishing useful precedents.

- Intermediaries should actively encourage and facilitate counter-speech and educational efforts in response to hate speech.

We think principles like these could provide a solid basis for an effective set of policies that would benefit practically everyone, including the vast majority of Internet users, companies that make a living on the web, and citizens concerned about the quality of our public discourse.

Beyond our Anti-Cyberhate Working Group, constructive dialogue about the best ways to encourage civility, tolerance, and respect online is under way in many quarters, with contributions from a range of participants.

Two of these participants are Danielle Citron and Helen Norton, two law professors whose 2011 article "Intermediaries and Hate Speech: Fostering Digital Citizenship for our Information Age" offers a number of proposals that echo the ideas of our Anti-Cyberhate Working Group. Citron and Norton call on Internet intermediaries to accept the responsibility of fostering "digital citizenship," which "aims to secure robust *and* responsible participation in online life." Here are some of the key principles they urge intermediaries to espouse:

- Strive for greater transparency about policies and definitions (for "hate speech," "speech that intentionally inflicts severe emotional distress," "speech that harasses," and other forms of offensive or dangerous content).

- Move more rapidly to block or remove hateful content and, when necessary, bar users who repeatedly post such content.
- Create more opportunities for counter-speech in response to hate speech, especially where children are affected.
- Educate and empower community users, including involving them in content decisions.
- Reshape websites' "architectural" choices and norms to encourage better behavior (for example, by discouraging anonymity in most circumstances).[19]

We don't necessarily endorse all these proposals, but we think they're very much the sorts of ideas that should be on the table when the problem of online hate speech is under discussion.

In a similar vein, Lori Andrews, a professor of law at the Illinois Institute of Technology's Chicago-Kent College of Law, has proposed what she calls a "Social Network Constitution" to define more clearly the rights and obligations of users, managers, and policymakers involved in online social media. Andrews is more concerned with issues like user privacy, cyber-bullying, and harassment than hate speech, but her discussion of issues such as due process, freedom of association, democratic self-determination, and transparency in the context of a program to establish fair rules for community life on the Internet illustrates the kind of joint effort we believe is necessary to move online governance to a higher level of sophistication, accountability, and fairness.[20]

Others have proposed specific initiatives that could help enable online communities to do a better job of policing themselves. In the wake of *The Innocence of Muslims* controversy in the fall of 2012, Tim Wu, a professor at Columbia University Law School, suggested that YouTube replace its current system, by which an anonymous team of staffers review and adjudicate flagged videos, with a community-based approach. In Wu's proposal, when "hard cases" of questionable content can't be quickly settled, "YouTube users of good standing—those that actually upload videos on a consistent basis—would be allowed to comment, until some kind of rough consensus is reached. Without consensus, the video stays. If this system worked, in the case of *The Innocence of Muslims*, someone could have made the case much earlier that the 'movie' should be taken down in Muslim countries as 'hate speech.'"

Wu recognizes that his proposed system could face both practical and theoretical difficulties. But he likens it to the community self-policing system that has worked reasonably well to maintain a high level of content on the online encyclopedia Wikipedia and suggests it's worth an experiment.[21] We'd be interested in the results of such an experiment—though we'd be concerned about the possibility that the online comment system might be "hijacked" by groups of people with an axe to grind. Could a neo-Nazi video producer whose program was "on trial" urge his followers to log into the online forum and provide supportive comments, thereby overwhelming and thwarting the will of the majority? The system would have to be carefully designed and monitored to prevent such an outcome.

∿

We're just two decades into the history of the Internet as a medium of mass communication. We've already seen amazing changes in its social, economic, and technological shape, and many more are surely on the horizon. Our goal as citizens who are concerned about the power of hatred to distort and destroy lives is to ensure that, as the Internet evolves, it will become ever more hospitable to civil, free, and open-minded exchanges of ideas—and an increasingly uncomfortable home for those whose purpose is to spread bigotry, lies, and hostility. The job will require a sustained commitment by activists, civic organizations, media and technology companies, government agencies, and especially ordinary citizens and users of the Internet. We hope every reader of this book will join in the effort.

WHEN GOOD MEN
DO NOTHING

Counter-Speech as the Antidote to Hatred

t the ADL, we believe that the best antidote to hate speech is counter-speech—exposing hate speech for its deceitful and false content, setting the record straight, and promoting the values of respect and diversity. To paraphrase U.S. Supreme Court Justice Brandeis, sunlight is still the best disinfectant. It is always better to expose hate to the light of day than to let it fester in the darkness, where it can grow and spread, nourished by ignorance and fear. For this reason, ADL devotes significant time and resources to educational programs for young people, who are the most impressionable, susceptible victims of hate speech.

Counter-speech—the dissemination of messages that challenge, rebut, and disavow messages of bigotry and hatred—can serve a wide variety of purposes, which we'll discuss in this chapter. Perhaps the most important is to simply provide irrefutable evidence to remind everyone that the world is full of people of good will—people who reject hatred and embrace the values of civility and respect.

This is a vitally important function in a world where the cacophony of communications media—especially the near-chaos of the Internet—can create a very different impression.

When conflict and extremism seize the headlines, voices of moderation and civility can easily be drowned out. The result is a misleading image of a world in which (in the words of the poet W. B. Yeats) "the best lack all conviction, while the worst / are full of passionate intensity." The reality is that many people who share our abhorrence for hate speech and our devotion to mutual respect also share our commitment to using the tools of modern communication to spread our positive message to the world. The existence of vigorous, robust channels of counter-speech helps to make this reality clear, allowing those who are undecided or susceptible to the siren song of bigotry to sense that there is a viable alternative.

For example, when television screens are filled with images of Muslims demonstrating or even rioting to protest disrespectful messages about their faith, we often hear Americans asking, "Where are the moderate Muslims calling for peace and mutual respect?" The implication is that the Muslim world is silent in the face of calls for violence against "infidels," which in turn fuels the assumption that today's world is divided into warring camps that are doomed to eternal, irreconcilable strife. This vision of a hostile planet continually on the brink of violence fuels further fear, paranoia, and hostility on all sides, making reconciliation and mutual understanding even more difficult to achieve.

The reality is that most Muslims, like most Christians and Jews, are peace-loving people who want to live in harmony with their neighbors. Counter-speech that highlights this reality (and removes the spotlight from the most extremist elements in Islam) is crucially important. Especially within the United States, there are many moderate Muslim leaders whose statements in support of religious and ethnic tolerance are rarely quoted in the mainstream media. Online columnist William Saletan recently presented a long list of comments from some of these leaders.[1] Here's just a small sampling:

> People of good will and good faith have to use their constitutional right to free expression to condemn incitement. . . . Freedom of speech applies to everybody. Once you start making exceptions, you start the erosion of the principle.—Rep. Keith Ellison (D-MN), first Muslim elected to Congress
>
> The answer to speech we find deeply offensive is more speech—speech that tells the true story of Islam—not censorship or violence.—Islamic Networks Group

> Muslims for Progressive Values upholds the principle of free speech, whether political, artistic, social or religious, even when that expression may be offensive and that dissent may be considered blasphemous. MPV holds that none should be legally prosecuted, imprisoned or detained for declaring or promoting unpopular opinions.—Muslims for Progressive Values

From time to time, we've strongly disagreed with Muslim leaders on particular issues, and ADL will certainly challenge them in the future when we consider it appropriate. But these quotations (and the many others cited by Saletan) suggest that the majority of Muslim leaders—along with leaders from every faith and ethnic community—share our understanding that free speech is a fundamental human right. At the same time, we join hands in deploring the evil of hate speech, and we're determined to combat it by speaking out against it as powerfully as possible. We join these Muslims of good will—as well as their counterparts in the Christian, Jewish, and other communities—in vowing to use the power of counter-speech to undercut the forces of hatred that threaten to divide us.

COUNTER-SPEECH FLOURISHES ON THE INTERNET

The cause of social tolerance is one in which the enormous reach of the Internet can serve as a weapon for good. In February 2008, Chris Wolf spoke on Internet hate speech in Jerusalem at the Global Forum Combating Anti-Semitism hosted by Israel's foreign minister, Tzipi Livni, and the minister of the Diaspora, Society, and Fight against Anti-Semitism.

Coinciding with the conference, Shimon Peres, the eighty-four-year-old leader of Israel, was addressing a group of international students. In his speech, Peres challenged young people to use their time on

Facebook to counter the spread of hate and bullying. Peres said, "Anti-Semitism is a disease of everyone. Persecuting minorities, discrimination, xenophobia and violence exist in many countries in the world. You have the opportunity to teach your friends about the memory of the Holocaust so that these horrors will never be forgotten and will never be repeated."

Peres is right about the power of viral speech online. If kids see their peers repeatedly speaking out against hate and intolerance, and reminding others of the effects of hate speech historically, it will make a difference—potentially a more effective difference than the enforcement of codes of conduct by website managers themselves.

Back in chapter one, we mentioned the horrific case of "Kill a Jew Day" on Facebook and the outpouring of anti-Semitic rants it provoked. But there's another, happier side to the story. The power of counter-speech was swiftly mobilized to show the world a widespread, dramatic response. Opponents quickly mounted a counter-event on Facebook titled "One Million Strong Against Kill a Jew Day." (Supporters actually numbered, more modestly, in the thousands.) And pursuant to the Facebook terms of service, complaints about the "Kill a Jew Day" event to Facebook administrators resulted in the company disabling the event page. This effective response to an outrageous offense against civility is a vivid example of the power of counter-speech as a vehicle for society to stand up against hate speech.

Hundreds of similar efforts to use counter-speech to expose, shame, and discourage hate speech have been mounted, addressing communities and problems large and small. For example, in May 2012, after a string of hate crimes occurred around the campus of Ohio State University, a group of students launched the @OSU_Haters Twitter account and the Tumblr account osuhaters.tumblr.com in an effort to "expose the hate at Ohio State." These social media accounts reprinted racist and otherwise biased tweets and images generated by Ohio State

students. Consolidating these scattered assaults in a single place produced an effect that was disturbing and provocative—deliberately so.
The goal: To spark a conversation among members of the Ohio State
community that reinforces the conviction that hatred has no place at a
great university.[2]

When it comes to counter-speech, even a single determined individual can have a notable impact. Hannah Jacobs is the mother of a
child who, like millions of others, is cognitively impaired and requires
special care. For Jacobs and her daughter, the word "retard" isn't just a
juvenile insult—it's hate speech that demeans and potentially threatens a human life. (Words like "nutcase," "whack job," and "moron" have
similar implications.) So when Jacobs discovered that hundreds of
webpages, includes many on Facebook, use "retard" as a routine term of
abuse, she decided to fight back. She created her own Facebook group
using the slogan "Stop Allowing Groups That Mock People with Special
Needs and Disabilities." Within a year it attracted 28,000 members. Jacobs also devotes part of her time every week to personally finding and
contacting people and groups with websites that abuse the disabled.
Many, who had been motivated more by ignorance than by true hatred,
agreed to alter or delete the offensive content. "It takes a lot of work,"
Jacobs says. But her goal is to use the powers of communication, reason, and persuasion to make the online world safer for people like her
daughter—and for everyone else who believes in civility and tolerance.[3]

An especially inspiring example of counter-speech is Wipeout Homophobia (originally known as Wipeout Homophobia On Facebook
[WHOF]). Based in Durham, England, WHOF originated precisely as
a response to hate-filled messages on the Internet and has since evolved
into a community of people supporting one another and their shared
vision of a more just and tolerant world. WHOF founder Kevin O'Neil
explains that the site was created after he stumbled upon a couple of
Facebook pages filled with anti-gay hatred. O'Neil flagged and reported

the pages to Facebook and sent links to a group of friends urging them to do the same:

> To cut a long story short, I thought that rather than 30 or so of us send-ing each other messages for the rest of the day, I would collate the links on one Facebook page, that way all of us could click report and if we felt like it we could invite friends to do the same. An hour later there were hundreds of members and by the end of that first day over a thousand like minded people had joined.[4]

When you visit WHOF on Facebook, you immediately discover that the page has grown into much more than a vehicle for protesting big-oted content on the social network. As of November 2012, the page has more than half a million "likes" and is filled with a constantly chang-ing array of news items, pictures, comments, and discussions posted by a huge number of friends and supporters, gay and straight alike. Young people questioning their sexual identity, those feeling scared of disapproval or hatred from their peers, and friends and family mem-bers wondering how to react to the news that a loved one is gay have all found WHOF a source of generous, honest, and non-judgmental information, contacts, and referrals for help. One can only guess at the number of young men and women who may have been lifted out of de-spair—and perhaps dissuaded from suicide—by the positive messages found at WHOF.

The site's origins as a response to hate speech still resonate. One of the most unusual features of WHOF is a page dedicated to samples of the hate mail that O'Neil has received—together with his replies. The gently sarcastic, highly literate style of the responses written by "Kel" (as O'Neil calls himself) contrasts vividly with the often incoherent, ob-scene vitriol of his correspondents—a contrast that, in itself, reinforces the message that a world driven by tolerance rather than hatred is a far more pleasant place to live. For example, one hater writes:

> you're kind makes me sick. don't you think there is enough crazy people in the world without spreading it to more people. the world would be better without gays and lessbeans and trannies and other disabilities. you need to delete your page before people see it and get annoid.

O'Neil's response:

Dear Darren,

Thank you for your lovely message, how nice of you to notice that I am Kind, I do try.

As for the subjects you wanted advice on—I'll do my best but believe me, I'm no oracle.

Yes I do believe that there are more than enough crazy people in the world, it always amazes me that people who wouldn't have been allowed crayons 10 years ago now have access to the internet. BTW what is your favorite colour crayon? Mine is blue, they taste best.

I doubt that the world would be better without gays; to be honest they would be a miss to the caring and service professions and don't even get me started on hair dressing.

Less beans would make the world a far worse place in my opinion, I love baked beans on toast and chili just isn't a chili without kidney beans—so I'll have to disagree with you there too.

I love my tranny, I listen to the BBC Radio 4 during the day for plays and comedies and discussions while I'm working, so I'd miss that a lot. Being gay isn't really a disability, unless you're a stud horse or a homophobic bigot, in which case I find that most homophobic bigots hide their latent homosexuality (*That means gayness*) and attack people who are openly gay so that they feel less insecure about themselves, but I don't need to explain that any further to you, do I?

Thank you for the excellent advice, my page, which has 400,000+ members, with MILLIONS of post views and website hits per month, will be deleted immediately; because we wouldn't want word to get out would we?

> Bye for now poppet, take care,
>
> love Wipe Out Homophobia xxx

Another gay-basher writes, "If you don't remove Wipe Out homophobia from Facebook I will make it my life's crusade to track you down and kill you. I have investigated you and I know who your mother is, she will be first on my list. You have 1 hour." To which O'Neil responds, "Well done on your investigative work, please remember to bring a shovel with you as my mother has been dead for 23 years." It's easy to see why O'Neil heads this often-hilarious page of the site with the warning, "Do NOT drink liquids over your keyboard whilst reading this page."[5]

Few people are capable of responding to hatred with as much sanity and good humor as Kevin O'Neil, and not everyone should even try. (As we'll discuss later in this chapter, there can be dangers in trying to engage bigots in direct counter-speech, even online, so this is an activity to be approached with caution.) Does the dialogue on WHOF succeed in turning the hearts and minds of anyone who approaches it with a preconceived attitude of homophobia? Perhaps not. But by empowering and encouraging voices of tolerance, counter-speech sites like this one help to marginalize the extremists and significantly impede their efforts to embolden supporters and intimidate opponents through the sheer volume and aggressiveness of their messages.

SPEAKING UP—HOW TO GET INVOLVED
AS A SOCIAL MEDIA MEMBER

Thankfully, there are significant numbers of people like Kevin O'Neil, Hannah Jacobs, and the organizers of One Million Strong who are willing to dedicate significant time and effort to launching social networking initiatives in response to hate speech. But not everyone is called to be an activist to the same extent. Many of us merely want some simple, effective ways to react when we encounter Internet contents that leave us feeling disgusted, threatened, or angry. When you find yourself in this position, here are some strategies you can use to fight back.

Flag the offensive content. As we discussed in chapter four, most social networking sites make it possible for users to flag offensive content for review. Most also allow you to say why you thought something was offensive.

On Facebook, for example, every page includes a link (which unfortunately is quite small and difficult to see) to "Terms," which refers to the "Terms and Policies" users must abide by when using Facebook. A further link connects you to "Facebook Community Standards," a page that describes in some detail nine kinds of "expression" that are subject to removal from Facebook pages.[6] These include violence and threats, self-harm (i.e., content that encourages suicide, self-mutilation, or "hard drug abuse"), bullying and harassment, hate speech, graphic content (defined as imagery that appeals to "sadistic pleasure"), nudity and pornography, identity and privacy, intellectual property (i.e., copyright infringement), and phishing and spam.

Hate speech, in turn, is defined in the Facebook community standards as speech that attacks a person "based on their race, ethnicity, national origin, religion, sex, gender, sexual orientation, disability or medical condition." As you can see, this is a fairly complete list of the most common forms of hate speech, all of which Facebook members are encouraged to flag and challenge.

Facebook's system for flagging content has evolved over time. Formerly, each post featured a small link labeled "Flag," which made it easy and obvious to see how to flag potentially abusive content. As of this writing, that ubiquitous link has been removed. Instead, you have to roll your mouse to the upper right hand corner of the post until a small X appears, along with the words "Report/Mark as Spam." Click on the X and you'll be led to a menu that reads:

All reports are strictly confidential. What best describes this?
- Spam or scam
- Sexually explicit content
- Hate speech or personal attack
- Violence or harmful behavior

If you choose the "Hate speech" option, you'll be given a further menu that lets you specify the particular form of hate speech, whether it targets you as an individual, a religious group, a race or ethnicity, and so on.

Other social networking sites—YouTube, Twitter, and others—have created their own flagging systems, each with its own procedures. Follow all the flagging steps currently provided on whichever social networking site you're visiting. The more information you provide, the better the chances that your complaint will be acted on swiftly and appropriately. If it's possible, make sure to include detailed comments as to why you thought the item was hateful.

Clarity is essential when communicating with Internet companies. They deal with thousands of complaints, so users need to explain exactly what has upset them, including a precise explanation of where the offensive content is located and why it is offensive even if it appears to be obvious. Do not assume that because you know that a certain word or idea or symbol is deeply troubling or offensive to you or your community that the person reviewing it knows that. Explain carefully, analytically, and with references if possible.

Finally, while this is less than ideal, it is reality: assume that the person who is reviewing your information has only a short period of time—seconds even—to consider your claim. Precision can go a long way to communicating your point. Complaints should be calm, polite, and to the point. Be clear and tell them exactly what you are asking them to do to remedy the situation. Specifically request a response, and copy a watchdog group such as the ADL on your communication.

Of course, there's no guarantee that the Facebook monitors will agree with your assessment of the content you find offensive. It's possible that it may remain online indefinitely. If that happens, you can take advantage of other opportunities to offer counter-speech that can have an important effect in mitigating the power of a hateful message.

Speak out. The beauty of social networking sites is that they are interactive. Everyone is capable of responding to content with content of their own, supportive or challenging. When you encounter material that promotes hate, post videos, comments, links to external content (such as the ADL website), or other materials that oppose the offensive point of view.

You may wonder whether a comment from a single person carries any weight in the vast universe of the Internet. It's important to let the social networking community see a competing perspective alongside the hateful one. Plenty of research shows that people are profoundly influenced in their attitudes, reactions, and behaviors by the perceived social context in which they operate. When it appears that no one is challenging a hateful message, it's easy for a vulnerable individual—a young person, someone with psychological problems, or an alienated loner—to assume that "everyone must feel this way" and so to be sucked into accepting the validity of a bigoted perspective. Even a single dissenting response can shatter that assumption and make it much easier for those visiting the page to heed "the better angels of our nature" rather than the devils of hostility that may be lurking within. And the appearance of one message of tolerance and respect often results in the posting of a second, a third, and then many others.

So speak out—you can never tell how great the impact of your positive message may be.

Applaud positive messages. Don't forget to post positive comments on content that shares positive messages. When you encounter websites or social media pages that offer ideas and information you find nurturing and supportive, add comments of your own, link to them on other sites, "like" or "friend" the positive pages, and recommend them to people you know.

Talk to others about what you've seen. When you encounter content that is troubling, frightening, or disturbing on the Internet, don't feel you need to deal with it on your own. It's generally easy to share the content with others who may be able to help—parents, teachers, friends, community or religious leaders, or the police. In addition to flagging the inappropriate material and reporting it to the Internet host responsible, you may want to alert others to the problem. Some web intermediaries have taken steps to facilitate this. For example, Facebook has created a system for social reporting that lets you send a copy of what you're reporting to a fellow Facebook user or anyone else with an email address. This system makes it easy for a young person, for example, to send a report about a problem to a parent, teacher, or other real-world presence. You can also notify groups, such as the ADL, which keep track of trends in hate speech. All of these are good approaches to counter-speech that help to shed a disinfecting light on the repulsive contents that are too commonly encountered on the Internet.

Think before you act. Perspective is crucial. Think before you respond, and try to respond in a thoughtful, careful manner.

There is a fine line between posting counter viewpoints and engaging extremists and haters in debate. We do not recommend that ordinary citizens try to engage extremists and haters in debate, either online or in a real-world forum. The atmospheres in which such "debates" are conducted are often emotionally charged, with audiences heavily weighted with fellow supporters of bigotry. Abusive language and even threats often replace reasoned dialogue. Logic and facts are ignored; instead, half-truths, distortions, and outright lies are presented that only a world-class expert is capable of unraveling and exposing. Under these circumstances, debating hatred is generally a losing proposition. Rather than engaging in debate, a link to a positive message or different point of view might suffice.

Dedicated hate websites hosting or welcoming anti-Semites, racists, neo-Nazis, Holocaust deniers, or other extremists are often not concerned if their rhetoric offends others. Complaints directly to these individuals will usually be unproductive. In some cases, a complaint may even provide satisfaction to the hate website owner and can provide the owner with your contact information and email address, subjecting you to unwanted hate email.

In other cases, exposure can have a positive impact by shaming purveyors of hate speech, especially when recognized community organizations, civic leaders, or government agencies play a role. John Mann is a member of the British parliament, a founder of the Interparliamentary Coalition for Combating Antisemitism, and chair of the British government's committee on dealing with anti-Semitism. Mann has spoken about how his committee has used social sanctions such as public exposure and humiliation and the threat of loss of employment to discourage and, where necessary, to punish serial offenders—individuals who have used the Internet repeatedly to harass and attack others because of their race, religion, or other characteristics. But Mann also notes that having the threat of legal sanctions as a backup is important to lend weight to these efforts, and to strengthen the hand of (for example) employers who might otherwise hesitate to fire a worker who has been promoting hatred on the Internet. As we've discussed, hate speech laws in the United Kingdom are significantly tougher than in the United States, which gives leaders like Mann a set of tools his American counterparts lack.

COUNTER-SPEECH BEYOND THE INTERNET

The issues of hate speech, freedom of debate, and our commitment to the First Amendment existed long before the rise of the Internet, and they remain important throughout our culture—in the mass media; in schools, universities, and religious institutions; within businesses and corporations; and in every aspect of local and community civil society. We all have an obligation to speak out against hate speech wherever we encounter it, whether on a social media network page or in a conversation among neighbors in the local diner.

This obligation also includes our responsibility, as citizens in a democracy, to play a fully informed role in the debates that reflect and shape attitudes about race, religion, ethnicity, sexual orientation, and tolerance. Counter-speech demands that we have the courage to label hate speech as such and refuse to help spread its virus. It also demands our readiness to thoughtfully examine, analyze, and publicly refute those more respectable arguments that serve to bolster the forces of bigotry and intolerance. Kenan Malik, a British writer and film-maker, has spoken eloquently about this responsibility:

In 2007, James Watson, the codiscoverer of the structure of DNA, claimed of Africans that their "intelligence is not the same as ours" and that blacks are genetically intellectually inferior. He was rightly condemned for his arguments. But most of those who condemned him did not bothering challenging the arguments, empirically or politically. They simply insisted that it is morally unacceptable to imagine that blacks are intellectually inferior. Britain's Equality and Human Rights Commission studied the remarks to see if it could bring any legal action. London's Science Museum, at which Watson was to have delivered a lecture, canceled his appearance, claiming that the Nobel Laureate had "gone beyond the point of acceptable debate." New York's Cold Spring Harbor Laboratory, of which Watson was director, not only disowned Watson's remarks but forced him eventually to resign.

I fundamentally disagree with Watson. Indeed I have written more than one book challenging such ideas, and have many times publicly debated their supporters. But I also think that it was as legitimate for Watson to have expressed his opinion as it is for me to express mine, even if I believe his assertion was factually wrong, morally suspect, and politically offensive. Simply to dismiss Watson's claim as beyond the bounds of reasonable debate is to refuse to confront the actual arguments, to decline to engage with an idea that clearly has considerable purchase, and therefore to do disservice to democracy.[7]

As a private, nonprofit organization, Cold Spring Harbor Laboratory of course has the right and the responsibility to make its own personnel decisions based on criteria it chooses, and it's understandable that it might prefer not to be guided by an individual whose thinking about race might bring discredit on the organization. The same logic applies to the London Science Museum, which is free to invite—or disinvite—public lecturers as it sees fit. But surely Malik is right that it's important for informed citizens to publicly challenge ideas like Watson's. To allow false statements that countenance and encourage bigotry to go unquestioned in the court of public opinion would make it that much easier for the real hatemongers—neo-Nazis, Klan enthusi-asts, and other racists who are obviously several notches below James Watson on any intellectual or moral scale—to mislead uninformed or impressionable people into believing that "science has proven the blacks are inferior." Providing vigorous counter-speech to rebut "sci-entific" (often pseudo-scientific) arguments in support of racism is a crucial job if we are to have an informed citizenry.

Of course, as we've noted, debating with closed-minded bigots is often a fruitless endeavor. Those who are wedded to hateful doctrines for their own emotional reasons are unlikely to be dissuaded by any factual arguments to the contrary, no matter how logical and irrefut-able. The resulting "debates" generate more heat than light, confusing less-informed members of the audience and frustrating those who believe in real intellectual engagement. It's not always easy to decide which opponents to engage publicly and which to simply expose as truly beyond the pale of civilized discourse. (It's a question that we at ADL are continually having to answer.) Unrepentant neo-Nazis like the organizers of Stormfront clearly fall on one side of the line, while Nobel Prize–winning scientists fall on the other. But this is a strategic issue every defender of freedom, civility, and tolerance must decide independently.

Nonetheless, it remains true that providing strong voices in oppo-sition to bigotry and hatred is one of the fundamental duties of every-one who cherishes democracy—and this applies both online and in any public forum where intolerance may rear its head.

Some counter-speech initiatives have been powerful enough to turn potentially divisive incidents into "teachable moments" that help to heal and unite communities. In September 2012, a self-proclaimed conservative organization called the American Freedom Defense Initia-tive launched a controversial advertising campaign in subway stations in New York City and Washington, D.C. The posters read, "In any war between civilized man and the savage, support the civilized man. Support Israel. Defeat Jihad."

Of course, everyone is entitled to an opinion about the ongoing conflict in the Middle East, and an ad campaign criticizing acts of terrorism against Israel (or any other country) would not have been controversial. But the American Freedom campaign offended many Americans by its use of the Muslim religious term "jihad" as synonymous with "terrorism" (a gross over-simplification at best) and its apparent equation of all (or most) Muslims with "savages." Even many strong supporters of Israel agreed that these posters stepped over the line, needlessly exacerbating already strained relations between Muslims and other Americans.

In both New York and Washington, subway officials initially rejected the ads, but courts subsequently ruled that American Freedom had the right to express its views and mandated that the ads be displayed.

In response, an effective counter-speech campaign was quickly launched. A Twitter offensive using the hashtag #MySubwayAd generated dozens of posts from ordinary citizens, such as "In NYC We Speak 140 Languages And Hate Isn't One Of Them," "We must meet the forces of hate with the power of love.—MLK Jr.," and ". . . and do not let the hatred of a people prevent you from being just.—Quran 5:8." Religious organizations also organized to buy advertising space in the same subway stations that displayed the anti-jihad posters. Shoulder to Shoulder, a coalition of twenty-eight religious groups including Christians, Muslims, and Jews, posted ads with the message, "Hate speech is not civilized. Support peace in word and deed." Sojourners, a liberal Christian organization, bought space for posters urging readers, "Love your Muslim neighbors." And the Council on American-Islamic Relations arranged to display ads in three metro stations quoting this verse from the Koran: "Show forgiveness, speak for justice and avoid the ignorant."

Counter-speech isn't only or even primarily about debating hate-mongers. It's about helping to create a climate of tolerance and openness for people of all kinds, not just on the Internet but in every aspect of local, community, and national life. Counter-speech in this sense includes public displays of support for embattled or isolated individuals or groups. It also includes gestures and activities that symbolize the willingness of a community to unite around values of inclusiveness and generosity. Counter-speech of this sort might include:

- A community "teach-in" with speeches, films, and playlets focused on the benefits of ethnic, racial, cultural, gender, and sexual inclusiveness.
- An annual street fair sponsored by local houses of worship that open their doors to share their music, food, customs, and traditions with those of different backgrounds.
- A town "book club" month in which an entire community joins in reading and discussing a book that thoughtfully expands people's understanding of varying ways of life.
- An "I Have a Dream" essay contest that encourages students to share and celebrate their unique perspectives on the American dream.
- A day of community service in which people visit blocks or neighborhoods different from their own to participate in fix-up or clean-up activities.
- A music or arts festival that could be timed to draw participants and media attention away from a potentially divisive events like a Klan rally or skinhead concert.
- A "Mix It Up at Lunch" day when school kids are urged to spend their cafeteria time eating and chatting with someone they never knew before.

Activities like these may not be "speech" in the traditional sense, but they speak volumes about the values of those who participate in them.

One of the organizations that has often fought alongside ADL in the battle against bigotry is the Southern Poverty Law Center (SPLC), based in Montgomery, AL. SPLC's booklet *Ten Ways To Fight Hate: A Community Response Guide* offers a number of wonderful examples of creative counter-speech used to undercut the messages of hatemongers. Here are just a handful of illustrations:

- Recognizing that the First Amendment protects the rights of hate groups like neo-Nazis to stage marches and rallies even in communities filled with minority-group members, Bill and Lindy Seltzer of Springfield, IL, devised a clever way to turn these activities against their perpetrators. Project Lemonade solicits pledges from individuals opposed to bigotry based on the number of minutes that a hate event lasts. The longer the hate rally, the bigger the fund amassed, thus transforming the "sour lemons" of hatred into something sweet and delectable. Monies raised are used for human rights projects, such as donating books on African American history to local libraries.

- When skinheads in Billings, MT, launched a campaign of harassment against local minority group members, local people fought back. After the Schnitzer family had a cinder block thrown through a window displaying a menorah, thousands of their neighbors bought and proudly displayed menorahs of their own as a gesture of solidarity. Other townspeople volunteered to repaint damaged houses and repair a vandalized cemetery. The outpouring of support led to a nationwide movement for community tolerance, dramatized in the movie *Not in Our Town*.

- When the Ku Klux Klan announced plans to boost their image by participating in the local Adopt-a-Highway program in Palatine, IL, local teenagers flooded City Hall with requests to join highway cleanup crews themselves. The youthful volunteers were so numerous they quickly took over every foot of highway available for the program, forcing the Klan members onto a waiting list.[8] In another case, the state of Missouri responded to the Klan's adoption of a stretch of highway by formally renaming it after civil rights pioneer Rosa Parks.

As these examples illustrate, counter-speech isn't just for those who are eloquent in public forums, skilled debaters, or graceful writers. Anyone who is willing to take a public stand against hatred can provide powerful counter-speech with an impact that may be difficult to quantify.

The great British conservative author Sir Edmund Burke one said, "All that is necessary for the triumph of evil is that good men do nothing." Don't let the failure to act be part of your personal legacy. When you see or hear evil, speak out against it. The difference you may make is incalculable.

"YOU'VE GOT TO BE CAREFULLY TAUGHT"

Education Is a Shared Responsibility

n addition to counter-speech, education is hugely important, because kids are the most impressionable, susceptible victims of hate speech.

In our pluralistic, multi-cultural society, public education has long been subject to social and political pressures. Discussions and debates about the need for educational reform in the United States generally center on such important issues as equality of opportunity for students no matter what neighborhood they grow up in or what school they attend; the need to improve American competitiveness in economically vital fields like science, math, and technology; the best ways to attract bright young graduates to the field of education; the proper balance in education between local control and national standards; and so on. Less frequently discussed, but equally important, is the crucial role of education in sustaining our national experiment in democratic self-government.

In a self-governing republic like the United States, ultimately political power rests in the hands of the citizens—that is, in our hands, collectively. Through the vote as well as through numerous other processes—political organizing, petitioning and lobbying, the court system, and especially the continual process of public debate—citizens shape and guide the actions of government, seeking to create the kind of country and society they choose to live in. Carrying out these processes of self-government effectively requires a particular set of skills, attitudes, and virtues, including civility, mutual respect, readiness to balance individual interests against societal needs, willingness to accept defeats in the political arena as well as in the marketplace of ideas, and commitment to the value of open debate and deliberation, even in the face of disappointments and (often heated) disagreements. As political philosopher Amy Gutmann has written:

> In practice, the development of deliberative character is essential to re-alizing the ideal of a democratically sovereign society. Democracy de-pends on a mutual commitment and trust among its citizens that the laws resulting from the democratic process are to be obeyed except when they violate the basic principles on which democratic sovereignty rests. Deliberative citizens are committed, at least partly through the inculca-tion of habit, to living up to the routine demands of democratic life, at the same time as they are committed to questioning those demands whenever they appear to threaten the foundational ideals of democratic sovereignty, such as respect for persons.[1]

These democratic virtues don't arise in people naturally and auto-matically. Instead, they must be nourished through education, broadly defined—including not just classroom teaching (though this is ex-tremely important) but also the education that takes place in families, in the interactions of people and groups in communities, in civic or-ganizations, and in the media. The combined impact of all these forces and others like them helps to shape the ideas, attitudes, and values of our citizens, either strengthening or weakening our shared commit-ment to democracy—which is perhaps the most crucial reason that education, in the fullest sense of the word, is a vital concern for every citizen.

For this reason, education about hate speech and its impact on the rights of citizens, the tenor of public discourse, and the future of our democracy is a challenge of growing importance in twenty-first-century America. Educating current and future generations about the relationship between hate speech and democracy will have a far greater positive impact than any set of laws that seek to govern or limit hate speech.

HATE SPEECH AND ACADEMIC FREEDOM

People sometimes wonder whether public schools and universities, as agencies of government, may prohibit the use of their computer services for the promotion of hate and extremist views. The answer is that public elementary and secondary schools and public universities must follow the First Amendment's prohibition against speech restrictions based on content or viewpoint. Nevertheless, court rulings and public policy decisions have made it clear that public schools and universities may take a number of specific steps to regulate speech that occurs on their premises. For example, they may:

- Promulgate rules for the use of their computer facilities that limit speech that is incompatible with the educational mission of the school. (See, for example, the case of *Tinker v. Des Moines Independent Community School District*, 393 U.S. 503, 514 [1969], which held that students retain First Amendment expression rights at school, which may be suppressed only if authorities reasonably "forecast substantial disruption of or material interference with school activities.")
- Set out reasonable policies for the prevention of cyber-bullying.
- Create content-neutral regulations that effectively prevent the use of school facilities or services for the dissemination of hate-filled contents. For example, a university may limit use of its computers and servers to academic activities only. This rule would likely prevent a student from creating a racist website for propaganda purposes or from sending racist emails from his student email account.

Many publicly supported colleges and universities have regulations along these lines, and courts have generally held that they are within their rights to do so. Thus, faculty members and administrators at public institutions of higher learning are not helpless when it comes to combating the threat of online hate among their students and other members of the campus community.

Private schools and universities generally have still greater freedom to create and enforce their own rules against hate speech. However, many private schools and universities make certain promises to users that might be legally binding, and it's clear that the rules they promulgate concerning campus communications must be vetted to be consistent with such promises. Moreover, some states, such as California, regulate how private schools govern students. For example, California Education Code Section 94367 says, "No private postsecondary educational institution shall make or enforce a rule subjecting a student to disciplinary sanctions solely on the basis of conduct that is speech or other communication that, when engaged in outside the campus or facility of a private postsecondary institution, is protected from governmental restriction by the First Amendment to the United States Constitution."

Within these broad constraints, however, many private colleges and universities have tackled the problem of hate speech as one of the challenges they need to address in pursuit of two, sometimes conflicting, goals. On the one hand, they need to uphold the traditional role of the college or university as a bastion of free inquiry, where a wide range of ideas, including those that are unpopular or controversial, may be openly examined and debated, in the belief that, over time, the most deserving truths will win out. On the other hand, they also strive to create an atmosphere that is conducive to truly free expression and learning—an atmosphere of mutual respect, tolerance, and acceptance, particularly in today's increasingly diverse, multi-ethnic, multi-religious, and multi-cultural society. Students and faculty must feel free to consider and express all manner of ideas—yet they must do so without creating an atmosphere of hostility or intimidation toward anyone, including those who may find particular ideas threatening or demeaning. This is the tightrope that today's college and university administrators need to walk.

Our view is that the tradition of free speech on campus is vitally important, both for colleges and universities themselves and for their role in helping to embody, maintain, and strengthen the flow of ideas from many perspectives, which is essential to a well-functioning democracy. Educational institutions should bend over backward to protect the rights of people representing a broad array of viewpoints to communicate their ideas freely. Even views that some may find distasteful, including political views from the far left and far right, deserve protection in an academic setting; they should not be subject to preemptive censorship by university authorities or to the "heckler's veto" represented by efforts to shout down particular speakers or prevent them from appearing through threats of violence.

This bias in favor of free speech, however, doesn't mean that colleges and universities are obligated to sponsor all kinds of speech. School administrators, departmental heads, program directors, and others in authority have both the right and responsibility to apply sound academic criteria and intellectual judgment when deciding whether to invite particular speakers, offer credentials or campus access to specific organizations, or hire or promote individual lecturers or teachers. Freedom of speech doesn't mean that a history department is obliged to hire a Holocaust denier to provide "balance" to its presentation of twentieth-century history, any more than a biology department would be required to hire a creationist to debunk the theory of evolution.

As always, context, judgment, and the details of a particular case are important and must be considered with care. A university is well within its rights to refuse to hire a lecturer whose criticisms of Israeli policy sometimes verge on outright anti-Semitism. But what if a student-run political organization chooses to invite that same lecturer to give a talk on campus? Depending on the circumstances, such a talk might be acceptable—particularly if the institution ensures that opposing points of view will be freely and fully presented. Whenever possible, erring on the side of greater freedom of speech—and taking full advantage of the power of counter-speech to enlighten, challenge, and educate—should be the guiding principle for educators.

The story of the now-defunct website JuicyCampus.com offers an instructive glimpse of the challenges facing university administrators, faculty, students, and other involved citizens in an age when the Internet makes it easy for every conceivable kind of message—including messages that are vicious and hateful—to invade college and university campuses, threatening the civility and openness of academic life.

Founded in the fall of 2007 by a young entrepreneur named Matt Ivester, JuicyCampus was an interactive campus-based website designed to traffic in gossip, rumors, and rants related to college life—the "juicier" the better. Initially targeting seven institutions (Duke University; Loyola Marymount University; the University of North Carolina; the University of Southern California; Pepperdine University; the University of California, Los Angeles; and the College of Charleston), JuicyCampus expanded within a year to over 500 campuses, attracting thousands of members and other visitors to its website.

Ivester claimed his goal was to provide an outlet for what he called "gossip 2.0," which he said could be "pretty entertaining," and the site's list of terms and conditions stated that material that was "unlawful, threatening, abusive, tortuous, defamatory, obscene, libelous, or invasive of another person's privacy" was not to be posted. (Hate speech is a notable omission from this list.) But JuicyCampus proudly proclaimed that it did no editing of posts, saying its mission was to enable "online anonymous free speech on college campuses."

In practice, the laxly enforced terms and conditions rules seemed to have little impact on the content of the site. Critics noted that the uncensored content of the site quickly came to include a wide range of personal attacks; sexist, racist, and homophobic slurs; obscene language and images; and threats of violence. Timothy Chester, chief information officer of Pepperdine University, described JuicyCampus as a "'virtual bathroom wall' for abusive, degrading, and hateful speech."[2] One day in March 2008, a researcher discovered these typical postings on JuicyCampus's main page:

D*** H**** You are mother f****** sl** a** fat hoe bag piece of sh**

Rich P***** is a f**

Philip V**** this guys is a f***** homo

Liz S**** easy to get into this asian slu** pants, hard part is getting her out, a couple of beers and this head case is easy for the picken

Hottest A** on Campus[3]

Some students claimed they were falsely identified as "cokeheads" or participants in pornographic videos on JuicyCampus, and they worried that these slurs would haunt them throughout their later life.

For reasons we've discussed throughout this book, seeking legal recourse against JuicyCampus would have been difficult. As we've seen, First Amendment protections of speech create high hurdles to possible lawsuits or criminal prosecutions, and Internet intermediaries are generally shielded from liability for the contents they publish by the provisions of the Communications Decency Act of 1996.

Instead, those offended by JuicyCampus found alternative ways of fighting back. One notable example is that of Pepperdine University, a California institution with a long-standing commitment to Christian values (for instance, the campus is "dry," forbidding the use of alcohol even by students old enough to meet legal requirements). In January 2008, Pepperdine's Student Government Association responded to widespread complaints about the site by voting 23–5 to ban JuicyCampus from university web servers, and it urged student groups at other universities to follow suit. (Several did.)

However, Pepperdine's student government doesn't have the power to block a legal website from university computers single-handedly. After the vote, the university created a committee that included several deans, the provost, and a member of the school's IT department to examine the question. In the end, this committee decided not to institute a ban against JuicyCampus, saying it feared that such an action would indicate "distrust of our students and a lack of appreciation for freedom of expression."[4] It urged students at Pepperdine to engage in dialogue about the hateful pockets of campus culture exposed by JuicyCampus, thereby transforming the negative power of the gossip site into a potential source for good.

The students responded with a classic counter-speech offensive. Mike Masten, a Pepperdine senior and a member of the student senate, helped launch the 429 Campaign, named after a Biblical passage (Ephesians 4:29) that advises, "Do not let any unwholesome talk come out of your mouths." The campaign culminated in a weeklong campus event focused on educating students about the hurt produced by thoughtless and hateful language.

Soon the backlash against JuicyCampus spread. Facebook groups with names like "BAN JuicyCampus," "Boycott JuicyCampus," and "Students Against JuicyCampus" began to proliferate. Google AdSense, which had provided major revenue to the site through its sale of advertisements, was inundated with complaints from students at Pepperdine and other colleges. In February 2008, Google severed its ties with JuicyCampus, forcing the company to shift to a smaller, less-well-known ad agency with less-restrictive content policies. Founder Matt Ivester said he was unconcerned, and traffic at JuicyCampus continued to rise.

In time, however, the negative publicity took a serious toll on Juicy-Campus's business aspirations. (An advertising downturn spurred by the recession of 2008–2009 didn't help matters.) In February 2009, the site shut down. Ivester issued a statement saying, in part, "In these historically difficult economic times, online ad revenue has plummeted and venture capital funding has dissolved. . . . While there are parts of JuicyCampus that none of us will miss—the mean-spirited posts and personal attacks—it has also been a place for the fun, lighthearted gossip of college life. I hope that is how it is remembered."[5]

Ironically, Ivester has since gone on to author a self-published book warning young people about the dangers of social media.[6] In an interview about the book, he talked about the JuicyCampus experience: "The site was out of control, and at 24, I simply didn't have the wherewithal or the experience to rein it in. . . . I felt trapped, unable to simply shut the site down—I had employees counting on me for their livelihood, and I had spent a lot of venture capital money with the expectation of a return on investment."[7]

The whole story of JuicyCampus vividly illustrates several of the major themes of this book: the ease with which hate speech online can spread and proliferate, harming individuals and poisoning the culture; the difficulty of "putting the genie back in the bottle" once the virus of hate has been unleashed; the difficult position in which college and university administrators find themselves when challenged to balance freedom of speech with the values of civility and tolerance; and, more hearteningly, the power of vigorous, intelligent counter-speech employed by those who are determined to fight back against the enablers of hate.

DIGITAL LITERACY AND HATE SPEECH

It's a national disgrace that we don't have as a requirement—in our elementary, middle school, and high school education—courses instructing children on the appropriate use of electronic communication. To start with, what kids do online can plague them for the rest of their lives. The Internet is a permanent record, and the contents essentially are available to anyone, anywhere. What kids say and do online can affect what schools they get into and what jobs they are offered. When kids reveal more than they should online, they risk their future and potentially their privacy and safety. Kids need to be taught the rules of online behavior.

And as to online hate, we're careful to warn our kids about the dangers they're likely to encounter in the real world, yet we don't do much to teach them how to protect themselves when they explore the online universe. Teaching kids how to filter the content they encounter online and separate bigoted speech from factual content, and teaching them why anti-Semitism, racism, and other forms of bias are woven from lies and hate, should be at the top of our digital literacy agenda. More fundamentally, rules of etiquette, ethics, and morality that are unique to the Internet should be taught to our kids, including the use of anonymity to engage in cyber-bullying and its close relation, hate speech.

There are only a few school systems in the country that require education in digital literacy. The historic decentralization of control over educational policies in the United States, the growing emphasis on testing in pursuit of improved classroom performance, the fear of controversy on the part of school administrators, and the politicization of many local school boards—all of these trends play a role in making this problem especially difficult to overcome.

Nonetheless, many of us who are concerned about the malignant power of hate speech are working to remedy this failing on the part of our educational system. For example, ADL has been involved in helping to craft a proposed Massachusetts law aimed at creating a school curriculum dedicated to Internet literacy. The statute would mandate that students should learn about how Internet activities can impact other people and also about categories of people most likely to be targeted, including, for example, members of racial or religious minorities and youngsters who identify as LGBT. These and other general principles would be defined and required by the legislation, with details to be worked out by the state department of elementary education within eighteen months of the law's passage. If this effort is successful, the Massachusetts law could become a model for similar legislation around the country.

We believe that education for coping with the challenges of digital life ought to be mandated, or at least made available, at the federal level through the Department of Education. It absolutely is fundamental not only to create a more civil society, but also to empower kids to protect themselves online, so that when they grow up they understand that certain words and behaviors are not acceptable. Meanwhile, school districts are free to adopt such programs as they see fit. ADL has many excellent resources, including curricula and programs, which deal with hate, prejudice, and violence, as well as such Internet-specific issues as cyber-bullying, and a large number of schools around the country are already using these materials with great success.

Within the field of digital literacy, students need to learn and master specific techniques for recognizing and responding appropriately to online hate speech. This challenge demands a number of intellectual and reasoning skills that, unfortunately, are not universally taught in American schools. They include:

- *An understanding of the importance of sources.* Who is behind a particular message, whether it is promulgated via the Internet or any other medium? What kind of bias or self-interested motive might underlie the message? Does the messenger have an obvious "axe to grind" that might skew or distort the ideas and facts presented? Are the messenger's apparent credentials—organizational affiliations, academic degrees or titles, lists of publications—meaningful or inflated and distorted? The fact that it's not always easy to identify the source of information on the Internet makes this particular digital literacy skill particularly important and challenging.

- *Recognition of bias.* The slanting of a message or of information may sometimes be obvious. For example, most students can recognize a racist tirade filled with hateful slurs ("nigger," "coon," and so on) for what it is. More often, and more insidiously, the bias may be expressed in far more subtle ways: through emotive language or images designed to trigger unconscious reactions that go deeper than the level of intellect; through careful selection of certain facts (and omission of others) that add up to a picture that may be accurate in detail but completely misleading in its totality; through use of linguistic, visual, and design cues that create a false impression of honesty, authority, and professionalism (such as "slick" webpage designs, official-sounding organization names, and apparently authentic photographic images); and through use of citations of and links to other sources that are biased in the same direction, in hopes that a sheer mass of such cross-references will create a "bandwagon effect" in the mind of readers.

- *A basic understanding of how the Internet works, including the role of search engines and social media networks as intermediaries and the interpretation of URLs.* The multiple layers of technology that constitute the Internet can make it dauntingly difficult for non-experts to trace the origins of particular material on the web. Fortunately, there are a growing number of online tools designed to help users disentangle the connections among websites, and students in digital literacy programs should be introduced to these. They include the "Who Is Registry" (www.internic.net /whois.html), which can often be used to trace the ownership and authorship of a particular website; the Alexa (www.alexa .com) web trafficking service, which shows how many visitors a particular site gets and provides some analysis about how that site relates to other sites; and the free software Touch Graph (www.touchgraph.com), which visually displays the relationship between links leading to and from a site.[8]

- *Ability to recognize the kinds of themes, motifs, and emotional appeals that are characteristic of hate-promoting organizations.* As noted by Mediasmarts, a Canadian nonprofit dedicated to digital and media literacy, "We need to teach youth to think critically about *all* the media they consume so that they can recognize hate in all its forms. Teaching young people about the ways that hate groups communicate their messages can help alert them to 'red flags' that show that someone is trying to manipulate them."

In its booklet *Responding to Online Hate*, Mediasmarts goes on to offer several examples of these "red flag" concepts:

- *The Other:* The most basic element of hate is the idea of "the Other"—a group that is seen as being completely different from the author's group, sometimes even portrayed as inhuman. The

Other is presented as being both inferior (to show that the author's group is superior) and threatening (to show that they are a danger to the author's group). Most hate groups are careful not to openly promote violence toward their targets. Instead, they create distorted histories and interpretations of current events to make readers believe that violence against the Other is justified.

- *The glorious past:* Another important element of hate is the idea that the group has fallen from its once-glorious past. This fall is shown as being the fault of the Other, and it is only by defeating and destroying the Other that this glorious past can be regained.
- *Victimhood:* Hate groups typically portray themselves, and the group they claim to represent, as victims of the Other. For example, white supremacist websites will claim that whites lose jobs or school placements, and even their own heritage, as a result of "reverse racism."[9]

Teachers of digital literacy should become familiar with these and other common motifs of hate sites so they can raise the sensitivities of their students to the presence of these seemingly harmless concepts and the sinister implications lurking just below the surface.

A fascinating illustration of the challenges of teaching digital literacy, particularly as it applies to hate speech, can be found in a study of how students react to and evaluate cloaked websites. The study was created and run by Jessie Daniels, a professor of sociology at the City University of New York and author of the book *Cyber Racism: White Supremacy Online and the New Attack on Civil Rights.*[10] As you'll recall from chapter one, cloaked websites present contents designed to promulgate hate under the guise of "educational" or "informational" material, thereby often luring students and other innocently curious web browsers into reading and perhaps accepting falsehoods as facts. Daniels, a leading expert on cloaked sites, recruited ten high school students to perform Internet searches on the topics of Martin Luther King, Jr., and the Civil Rights movement, "as if you had a report to write for school." Then he or an assistant watched the students in action, recorded the sites they visited, and asked them questions about their reactions.

The results were eye-opening. In every search, the cloaked sites www.martinlutherking.org and www.AmericanCivilRightsReview .org—both hate sites masquerading as objective sources of information—were among the first sites listed in the Google results. This alone led students to assume that these sites were probably legitimate; as one sixteen-year-old student remarked, "There must be a reason why everything's on the first page and the rest of the stuff is later." The "reason," of course, is the complex and frequently updated proprietary algorithm that Google uses to determine search rankings. This algorithm does *not* reflect any attempt to judge the accuracy or authority of sites, but many students (and other users) assume it does, which is a profound and potentially dangerous misunderstanding of how the Internet conveys information.

Other common forms of "digital illiteracy" among the students Daniels interviewed were almost equally serious. Some students, who apparently had been taught to evaluate the URL of a website as a way of gauging its authority (in itself a potentially useful strategy), jumped to the conclusion that www.martinlutherking.org was a reliable site simply because of its .org suffix, which they assumed marked the site as "unbiased" and "authoritative." Others reacted to the presentation of photos on the sites as if these lent authenticity; as one eighteen-year-old commented, "This site looks good, I mean, it has a lot of pictures and photos so you can see for yourself what happened." (Of course, in the era of Photoshop, more sophisticated data consumers understand that a photo doesn't necessarily constitute reliable evidence of "what happened.")

Even students who had been trained to be sensitive to the presence of bias didn't necessarily know how to apply that sensitivity in specific cases. For example, one seventeen-year-old student who visited the official website of the King Center Atlanta (www.thekingcenter.org) decided that it might not be a reliable source of information about Dr. King by reasoning, "Well, you know, in looking at this site, it appears to be created by his widow, or his family, so, it could be biased." By contrast, a different student who visited the cloaked hate site dedicated to impugning King noted a book by notorious Ku Klux Klan leader David Duke as merely one of a collection of books about Dr. King "by other people." (When the researcher asked this student if she knew who Duke was, she replied, "No, I have no idea.")

Of course, in a literal sense, it is true that the presentation of Dr. King's life and legacy approved by his widow, Coretta Scott King, is likely to be "biased" in a positive direction, just as the presentation created by a Klan leader is likely to be biased in a negative direction; but by virtually any measure, there's no doubt which of these two sources of information is likely to be more accurate. Many students, it appears, are ill-equipped to recognize this difference.[11]

Daniels's research suggests how far we have to go to ensure that our young people are fully equipped to understand the nature of the online world in which they are wandering, and how complex are the detailed skills they need to develop in order to be secure against victimization by digital purveyors of hate.

BEYOND THE CLASSROOM: WHAT PARENTS AND GUARDIANS CAN DO

Important as classroom teachers and curricula are, most young people spend far more of their online time at home, which means that parents and guardians play a critical role in ensuring that viral hatred does not infect their children. Here are some of the things that parents and guardians need to do to help their kids avoid the pitfalls waiting in the shadows of the Internet:

- Teach your children to use electronic communications in a safe and responsible manner.
- Prepare your children to identify cyber-bullying and hate speech when they see it.
- Talk with your children about their online activities so they don't become passive victims of cyber-bullying, online threats, harassment, or hate speech.
- Ensure that your children are not perpetrators or participants in cyber-bullying or the spread of online hate speech.
- Report any efforts made to target children for cyber-bullying or online bigotry to web service providers, law enforcement, school officials, and/or watchdog agencies such as the ADL, as appropriate.
- Work to ensure that schools and school districts have appropriate anti-cyber-bullying and anti-hate speech policies in place, for example, through your PTA.
- Speak out—and make sure school officials speak out consistently and forcefully—against hate and bigotry.

Of course, for parents to play their vital educational role effectively, it's essential for them to educate themselves about the online world. Even if you're not personally caught up in the world of social media, devote some time to learning about the most popular sites—Facebook, Twitter, YouTube, and the like—particularly those your children may be involved in. Most of these social networks have rules restricting participation by young people—for example, the current policy of Facebook prevents anyone younger than thirteen from opening an account—but the rules are relatively easy to skirt. (One study found that fifty-five percent of families with a twelve-year-old child reported that the youngster had a Facebook account—and that in most cases the parents themselves had helped set up the account.[12]) Visit the sites, spend some time navigating them, read their rules and conditions of participation, and sample the contents of a variety of pages. And talk with other parents about the things they see online. The world of the Internet is vast and ever-changing, requiring continual vigilance by those responsible for children.

Many of the social networking sites provide help pages and other forms of advice and guidance for parents, and online gaming sites are also making efforts to reach out to parents. Microsoft, for example, has created an educational site called Get Game Smart (http://www.get-gamesmart.com/) that offers information, activities, tools, and advice for families and parents on how to make sure that gamers can feel safe and comfortable when playing online. Sources like these can provide valuable fodder for the crucial educational conversations that only parents are positioned to have with their children.

Of course, talking about prejudice and hatred can often be challenging for parents, just as it is for professional educators. Strong emotions are involved, and kids with limited experience or understanding may say things that provoke intense reactions on the part of parents and other adults. You may find yourself in a situation where the proper ways to react aren't completely clear—for example, when talking with young friends of your children who come from a different social, ethnic, or religious backgrounds, or when interacting with young people in a church or synagogue group, a Scout or other youth organization, or just in the neighborhood.

Educator Lee Warren recounts an incident that is typical of the kind of encounter that is apt to occur when racial, social, or religious prejudices are under discussion. A young college teacher of African American studies was leading a discussion of the Black Muslim leader Louis

Farrakhan. When a female Jewish student remarked, "Only uneducated black men would believe in Farrakhan," she was angrily denounced by half a dozen black males in the class. She fled the classroom in tears.

Fortunately, the teacher was both tenacious and sensitive. He pursued the Jewish student and urged her to return to class, saying that it was important to understand why thoughtful black college students might find Farrakhan's teachings attractive. And he told the black students that it was equally important for them to understand why a white person might consider Farrakhan unworthy of respect. The result was a honest dialogue that the entire class benefited from. Warren concludes, "This young man was able to turn a hot moment into a profound learning opportunity for his students. He did it by keeping his head, not taking sides, and letting both groups know that they would gain immeasurably by understanding the arguments of the other side.[13]

At ADL, we've long been critical of Louis Farrakhan and his racially charged appeals to African Americans. We consider him a divisive figure who has harmed relations between the races rather than helped them. But a college course in African American studies is the perfect venue for young Americans, black and white, to come together to learn about such an influential figure, examine his impact (for good or evil), and share differing perspectives on him. The young teacher in Warren's story is to be commended for his skill in turning a moment of confrontation, hurt, and anger into an opportunity for learning and deeper understanding across both sides of an uncomfortable racial divide. All of us who want to help participate in the positive education of our young people around the volatile issues of prejudice, bigotry, and hate need to strive to develop similar qualities of sensitivity, tenacity, and poise.

Warren's article, while intended for teachers, offers a number of practical suggestions that can be helpful to any adult who finds himself or herself talking about these topics with young people. They include:

- *Listen for the subtext.* People often don't articulate clearly the tangle of emotions, experiences, and thoughts that underlie the words they use. When a young person makes a remark that sounds uninformed, hostile, or even hateful, stop the conversation to ask why. What is the source of the statement? Where did the idea come from? A discussion of the root causes of bias can be more rewarding—and more enlightening—than simply condemning it.

- *Shift the conversation from the personal to the impersonal.* Rather than forcing a young person to defend something he or she has said, put the idea on the table for everyone to discuss, using a framing statement such as, "Many people think this way. Why do they hold such views?"

- *Encourage participants in the discussion to really listen to and understand one another's perspectives.* When a conversation moves into "debate" mode, people begin to focus on scoring points and "winning" the argument rather than on learning from one another.

- *Don't take the discussion personally.* As the adult in the room, you may feel that some of the remarks uttered are directed against you personally. Try not to take them that way. Distance yourself from your own emotional reactions, take a deep breath, and try to explore the topic objectively rather than simply react.

- *Know yourself.* We all have biases, whether we fully recognize them or not—"hot buttons" that cause us to react with anger, hurt, or disdain. Get to know your own assumptions about people and think carefully before expressing them.

EDUCATION AS A BULWARK OF FREEDOM

As we conclude this chapter on education, let's recall the theme with which it started: the vital importance of education in supporting and strengthening our national commitment to democracy. Teaching our young people, and others, about the dangers of hate speech and the virtues of tolerance and respect isn't just about protecting minorities or "outsiders" from being victimized or abused. It's about reaffirming the values that are essential to a functioning system of self-governance.

In a sense, this argument about self-governance reinforces our conviction that laws attempting to prohibit hate speech are probably one of the weakest tools we can use against bigotry. There's no question that hate speech, which includes threats, harassment, incitements to violence, and other criminal actions unprotected by the First Amendment, should be subject to legal sanction. But broader regulation of hate speech may send an "educational message" that actually weakens rather than strengthens our system of democratic values. As legal scholar Robert Post has argued, such regulation

> not only sends a message of intolerance—that those who believe certain ideas are not welcome within processes of public opinion formation—but it also undercuts democratic legitimation with respect to such persons. It stands as an open invitation to exclude from public-opinion formation those who hold views that a majority believes should be beyond the pale. These are very dangerous and costly moves in a democracy.[14]

Teaching respect is everybody's business—and it's a more potent tool for vanquishing the hatemongers than the blunt instrument of law.

7

PROMOTING CIVILITY AND REDUCING HATE ON THE INTERNET

We think everyone who shares our concern about online hate should accept responsibility for defining and defending norms of civil behavior—not just on the Internet, but throughout society.

Back in 1961, Federal Communications Commission chairman Newton Minow famously referred to television as "a vast wasteland," attempting to shame the (then) three networks into improving the quality of the content they were broadcasting. Today, the Internet is in a similar state. As television was in the 1960s, the Internet is a universe filled with incredible promise, pockets of amazing brilliance and creativity, and vast disappointing stretches focused on pornography, conspiracy-mongering, hate speech, and other offensive materials.

The difference between broadcast TV and the Internet, however, is that all of us contribute to the flood of materials online. We can help influence, if not control, the online universe—and we need to start making a conscious effort to move its content in the direction of civility, respect, and tolerance. Several fundamental principles need to be more widely recognized, understood, and followed.

What you do online can hurt people. Despite the adage about sticks and stones, words can and do hurt—especially when anyone can publish information that reaches millions.

At a minimum, hate speech is online pollution, but it can go much further. It reinforces stereotypes and strengthens the belief that singling out "the other" for abuse is acceptable. Hate speech can harden low self-esteem and intimidate its targets—and even lead people to commit suicide, as the Tyler Clementi–Dharun Ravi case reminds us.

Online bystanders have a responsibility. Some students in the Rutgers dorm were amused by Ravi's spycam-Twitter scheme. Others ignored it. They should have been outraged, and they should have done something about it. "If you see something, say something" is not an admonition restricted to the security realm.

Tools are online for each of us to flag and report content that is objectionable. Most online companies have staffs to review such reports and to take action, from removing the offensive content to ejecting the person who posted it. Each of us should take responsibility to combat hate-filled content.

Speak up. Clicking to report hate speech to an online host is not all we can do. Hate speech legitimizes discrimination and even violence, and many of the people who post it do so, at least in part, because they believe no one objects. So object. Speak up to counter the lies of hate speech or the inappropriate online conduct directed at minorities. Just as the Internet provides thoughtless haters with broadcasting tools, each of us has those same tools at our disposal. A little counter-speech can go a long way.

Counter-speech is not censorship. People who misunderstand the great American tradition of freedom of speech sometimes talk as if criticism—especially harsh criticism—is tantamount to censorship. Of course it is not. Freedom of speech doesn't include freedom from disagreement or even public rebuke—and those who peddle hate speech deserve public rebuke, ridicule, and condemnation.

Privacy is a shared responsibility. Discussions about privacy usually revolve around consumer privacy and protection or government access to private content. But in this era of social media, when everyone can be a publisher and broadcaster, individual responsibility to respect privacy should also be a focus. Most people know that secretly setting up a webcam to spy on someone is wrong. But posting embarrassing photos and videos and making thoughtless comments can be a wrongful invasion of privacy as well. Each of us has a responsibility to consider the privacy implications for others of what we do online. Invading someone's privacy can have hateful effects.

Hatred is not funny. Finally, while young people today are much more accepting of gay people, an undercurrent of homophobia remains. Dharun Ravi most likely would not have set up a webcam to catch his roommate making out with a girl, nor would he have tweeted about it.

In some quarters, the put-down "That's so gay" is still common parlance. Many think of gays and lesbians as "the other" and as fair game for jokes. Racist and anti-Semitic jokes still have currency. Ravi may have thought what he was doing to his roommate was funny, but he now knows it was anything but, for Clementi and for himself.

The good news is that social norms and pressure do work. In social media, we see people reacting to what others say, and we see that this can have a tempering impact. More people need to react to hate speech rather than giving it a pass.

Let's take back responsibility for our culture—both online and off. Public involvement, concern, action, and, when necessary, outcry are key. Society must impose informal sanctions on those who facilitate the spread of hatred. If we do this, then those who would use the power of electronic communication to sow dissension, hatred, and violence in our society will once again be relegated to the darkest, least-frequented corners of our world—where they belong.

Appendix A

DEFEND FREE SPEECH, FIGHT HATE SPEECH

By Abraham H. Foxman

This article originally appeared in Haaretz on September 25, 2012.

The anger and the violence that raged around the anti-Islamic film trailer [for *The Innocence of Muslims*] on YouTube leads to a number of reactions. First, one should not forget the almost hair-trigger resort to violence in extremist Islamic circles, of which the anti-Western attacks on U.S. missions in Libya and Egypt are just a small part. Almost every day in some corner of the Islamic world, Muslims are attacking Muslims for their religious beliefs, Sunnis vs. Shia and vice-versa, including attacks on mosques and on religious holidays. The focus, therefore, needs first to be on the violence resulting from this culture of religious intolerance, of which anti-Western rage is just one manifestation. Violence is never an acceptable reaction. Beyond that, however, is the profound question of the right of free expression against the right not to be defamed. As the director of the Anti-Defamation League, an organization whose number one priority is to combat anti-Semitism, these values can at times appear to be competing, are greatly challenging and not always simple to decipher.

In the United States, we see the protection of free speech under the First Amendment of the Bill of Rights as a core value of a thriving democracy. Free speech has also proven to be especially important for those in the religious minority, particularly Jews, in the United States. It is perhaps not a coincidence that the First Amendment protects not only free speech, but also the freedom of religion. Those provisions, taken together, have enabled people of many faiths and of no faith to thrive in America, free from government interference. And they have been singularly important for American Jews. Freedom of speech, universally accepted, has been a great force for equality, for non-discrimination, and for justice.

But freedom of speech in America is also more than a right; it carries with it a serious responsibility. For the marketplace of ideas to work—indeed for democracy to work—those who see and hear speech that they believe is offensive or hateful must be willing and ready to exercise their own free speech rights in response. They must stand up for others who are less capable of standing up for themselves. And this is really true of any democracy. A democracy does not work if people are not engaged, and to be engaged, people must have the freedom to express themselves. Leaders everywhere have the added responsibility of educating others by their own example to become engaged in speaking out against expressions of hate. This works in America because of our history, our pluralism, our constitutional system and because the public has been educated on the idea that the best way to fight hate speech is with good speech and exposure.

Of course, for us at the ADL we have other methods of dealing with hate, including monitoring and exposing hate groups, demanding that leaders, like presidents of universities, speak up against haters on campus, and when it moves from speech to action, by hate crime laws. We recognize at the same time, however, that the American experience and system are unique. When it comes to Europe, Israel and elsewhere, we are not so quick to try to impose our way of thinking on very different societies.

In Germany and elsewhere, with the tragic history of massive anti-Semitism, laws banning swastikas and anti-Semitic statements are common. There is recognition that the free speech standard that exists in America is not the norm for Europe. And while we are proud of our system, we accept that a less strict boundary between speech and action may be more appropriate elsewhere. Indeed, in Israel, too, there is greater inclination to ban certain types of incendiary hate speech. At this point, I am reluctant to say that we have it right and Israel and the Europeans do not. Rather I would say that for America it is the law, protected by the courts, and it has largely worked to the benefit of all, including Jews.

For Israel, for Europe, other approaches are necessary. There is not a First-Amendment-like tradition in these societies, and therefore it is unlikely that a purist position could be adopted when people are outraged by hate speech.

On the other hand, countries that put restrictions on speech should be constantly on the alert to make sure that these are narrowly tailored and do not become an excuse for limiting free expression.

As Jews, we know better than most how devastating words of hate can be. But we also know how equally devastating can be a process in which free expression is restricted under the guise of avoiding certain kinds of hate. On college campuses in the United Kingdom, there are efforts to ban pro-Israel activities because they are deemed hateful.

As long as we keep in mind the need both to provide true free expression while still speaking up and encouraging others to join the effort against hate speech, the dilemma that these two matters raise can be overcome.

Appendix B

RESPONDING TO EXTREMIST SPEECH ONLINE

Ten Frequently Asked Questions

A convenient summary of basic information about legal and practical considerations regarding the response to extremist speech on the Internet, from the ADL website.

As an organization dedicated to the eradication of bigotry in all its forms, the ADL has long been concerned about the propagation of racism, anti-Semitism, and prejudice on the Internet. After all, this medium allows extremists easy access to a potential audience of millions. In numerous reports, the ADL has detailed the ways bigots are using the Internet to promote and recruit for their cause, communicate more easily and cheaply, and reach new audiences—particularly the young. The Internet offers both propaganda and how-to manuals for those seeking to act out fantasies of intolerance and violence.

Practically and legally, combating online extremism is enormously difficult. The First Amendment's protection of free speech shields most extremist propaganda, and Internet Service Providers, the private companies that host most extremist sites, may freely choose whether to house these sites. When providers choose not to host hateful sites, these sites migrate easily to the computers of services without such restrictions. Furthermore, the size of the web, which contains hundreds of millions of distinct pages, complicates efforts to identify extremist material. Hundreds if not thousands of webpages, some of which are not listed by search engines, contain bomb-making formulas.

There are no simple answers. Yet, we as a society must find a way to respond to this daunting challenge. We need to recognize warning signs like the existence of the websites attributed to the Littleton suspects. Internet users need to let responsible authorities know about the threatening, hateful, and violent material they find. And the computer industry, educators, parents, civil rights groups, and government agencies must work together to develop new and creative approaches to the unprecedented challenges posed by online extremism.

This document answers ten frequently asked questions regarding regulation of hate on the Internet.

1. Why can't the government ban use of the Internet to spread hateful and racist ideology in the United States?

The Internet is probably the greatest forum for the exchange of ideas that the world has ever seen. It operates across national borders, and efforts by the international community or any one government to regulate speech on the Internet would be virtually impossible, both technologically and legally.

In the United States, the First Amendment to the Constitution guarantees the right of freedom of speech to all Americans, even those whose opinions are reprehensible. In a number of recent decisions, the Supreme Court has reaffirmed that our government may not regulate the content of Internet speech to an extent greater than it may regulate speech in more traditional areas of expression such as the print media, the broadcast media, or the public square. While courts may take into account the Internet's vast reach and accessibility, they must still approach attempts to censor or regulate speech online from a traditional constitutional framework.

2. **What kind of hate speech on the Internet is not protected by the First Amendment?**

Internet speech that is merely critical, annoying, offensive, or demeaning enjoys constitutional protection. However, the First Amendment does not provide a shield for libelous speech or copyright infringement, nor does it protect certain speech that threatens or harasses other people. For example, an email or a posting on a website that expresses a clear intention or threat by its writer to commit an unlawful act against another specific person is likely to be actionable under criminal law. Persistent or pernicious harassment aimed at a specific individual is not protected if it inflicts or intends to inflict emotional or physical harm. To rise to this level, harassment on the Internet would have to consist of a "course of conduct" rather than a single isolated instance. A difficulty in enforcing laws against harassment is the ease of anonymous communication on the Internet. Using a service that provides almost-complete anonymity, a bigot may repeatedly email his victim without being readily identified.

Blanket statements expressing hatred of an ethnic, racial, or religious nature are protected by the First Amendment, even if those statements mention individual people and even if they cause distress in those individuals. Similarly, denial of the Holocaust—though abhorrent—is almost never actionable under American law. The Constitution protects the vast majority of extremist websites that disseminate racist or anti-Semitic propaganda.

3. **Has anyone ever been successfully prosecuted in the United States for sending racist threats via email?**

There is legal precedent for such a prosecution. In 1998, a former student was sentenced to one year in prison for sending email death threats to sixty Asian-American students at the University of California, Irvine. His email was signed "Asian hater" and threatened that he would "make it my life career [*sic*] to find and kill everyone one [*sic*] of you personally." That same year, another California man pled guilty to federal civil rights charges after he sent racist email threats to dozens of Latinos throughout the country.

4. **Has anyone ever been held liable in the United States for encouraging acts of violence on the World Wide Web?**

Yes. In 1999, a coalition of groups opposed to abortion was ordered to pay over $100 million in damages for providing information for a website called

"Nuremberg Files," which posed a threat to the safety of a number of doctors and clinic workers who perform abortions. The site posted photos of abortion providers, their home addresses and license plate numbers, and the names of their spouses and children. In three instances, after a doctor listed on the site was murdered, a line was drawn through his name. Although the site fell short of explicitly calling for assault on doctors, the jury found that the information it contained amounted to a real threat of bodily harm.

5. Can hate crimes laws be used against hate speech on the Internet?

If a bigot's use of the Internet rises to the level of criminal conduct, it may subject the perpetrator to an enhanced sentence under a state's hate crimes law. Currently, forty states and the District of Columbia have such laws in place. The criminal's sentence may be more severe if the prosecution can prove that he or she intentionally selected the victim based on the victim's race, nationality, religion, gender, or sexual orientation. However, these laws do not apply to conduct or speech protected by the First Amendment

**6. May commercial Internet Service Providers (ISPs)
prevent the use of their services by extremists?**

Yes. Commercial ISPs, such as America Online (AOL), may voluntarily agree to prohibit users from sending racist or bigoted messages over their services. Such prohibitions do not implicate First Amendment rights because they are entered into through private contracts and do not involve government action in any way.

Once an ISP promulgates such regulations, it must monitor the use of its service to ensure that the regulations are followed. If a violation does occur, the ISP should, as a contractual matter, take action to prevent it from happening again. For example, if a participant in a chat room engages in racist speech in violation of the "terms of service" of the ISP, his account could be cancelled, or he could be forbidden from using the chat room in the future. ISPs should encourage users to report suspected violations to company representatives.

The effectiveness of this remedy is limited, however. Any subscriber to an ISP who loses his or her account for violating that ISP's regulations may resume propagating hate by subsequently signing up with any of the dozens of more permissive ISPs in the marketplace.

**7. May universities prevent the use of their computer
services for the promotion of extremist views?**

Because private universities are not agents of the government, they may forbid users from engaging in offensive speech using university equipment or university services. Public universities, as agents of the government, must follow the First Amendment's prohibition against speech restrictions based on content or viewpoint.

Nonetheless, public universities may promulgate content-neutral regulations that effectively prevent the use of school facilities or services by extremists. For example, a university may limit use of its computers and server to academic activities only. This would likely prevent a student from creating a racist website for propaganda purposes or from sending a racist email from his student email account. One such policy—at the University of Illinois at Champaign-Urbana—stipulates that its computer services are "provided in support of the educational, research and public service missions of the University and its use must be limited to those purposes."

Universities depend on an atmosphere of academic freedom and uninhibited expression. Any decision to limit speech on a university campus—even speech in cyberspace—will inevitably affect this ideal. College administrators should confer with representatives from both the faculty and student body when implementing such policies.

8. **How does the law in foreign countries differ from American law regarding hate on the Internet? Can an American citizen be subject to criminal charges abroad for sending or posting material that is illegal in other countries?**

In most countries, hate speech does not receive the same constitutional protection as it does in the United States. In Germany, for example, it is illegal to promote Nazi ideology. In many European countries, it is illegal to deny the reality of the Holocaust. Authorities in Denmark, France, Britain, Germany, and Canada have brought charges for crimes involving hate speech on the Internet.

While national borders have little meaning in cyberspace, Internet users who export material that is illegal in some foreign countries may be subject to prosecution under certain circumstances. An American citizen who posts material on the Internet that is illegal in a foreign country could be prosecuted if he subjected himself to the jurisdiction of that country or of another country whose extradition laws would allow for his arrest and deportation. However, under American law, the United States will not extradite a person for engaging in a constitutionally protected activity even if that activity violates a criminal law elsewhere.

9. **What are Internet "filters" and when is their use appropriate?**

Filters are software that can be installed along with a web browser to block access to certain websites that contain inappropriate or offensive material. Parents may choose to install filters on their children's computers in order to prevent them from viewing sites that contain pornography or other problematic material. ADL has developed a filter (ADL HateFilter™) that blocks access to websites that advocate hatred, bigotry, or violence toward Jews or other groups on the basis of their religion, race, ethnicity, sexual orientation, or other immutable characteristics. HateFilter™, which can be downloaded from ADL's website, contains a "redirect" feature that offers users who try to access a blocked site the chance to link directly to related ADL educational material. The voluntary use of filtering software in private institutions or by parents in the home does not violate the First Amendment because such use involves no government action.

There are also some commercially marketed filters that focus on offensive words and phrases. Such filters, which are not site-based, are designed primarily to screen out obscene and pornographic material.

**10. May public schools and public libraries install filters
on computer equipment available for public use?**

The use of filters by public institutions, such as schools and libraries, has become a hotly contested issue that remains unresolved. At least one federal court has ruled that a local library board may not require the use of filtering software on all library Internet computer terminals. A possible compromise for public libraries with multiple computers would be to allow unrestricted Internet use for adults, but to provide only supervised access for children.

Courts have not ruled on the constitutionality of hate speech filters on public school library computers. However, given the broad free speech rights afforded to students by the First Amendment, it is unlikely that courts would allow school libraries to require filters on all computers available for student use.

Appendix C

SUNDAY DIALOGUE

Anonymity and Incivility on the Internet

A letter from Christopher Wolf proposing that Internet intermediaries should consider requiring content posters to provide their real names, together with a number of thoughtful responses from readers and a final observation by Wolf. From the New York Times, *November 26, 2011, © 2011, The New York Times.* All Rights Reserved. Used by permission and protected by the Copyright Laws of the United States. The printing, copying, redistribution, or retransmission of the Material without express written permission is prohibited.

THE LETTER

To the Editor:

Facebook has 800 million users who are required to use their real names ("Naming Names: Rushdie Wins Facebook Fight," front page, Nov. 15), and, as a result, are identified with and accountable for what they post. It is time to consider Facebook's real-name policy as an Internet norm because online identification demonstrably leads to accountability and promotes civility.

People who are able to post anonymously (or pseudonymously) are far more likely to say awful things, sometimes with awful consequences, such as the suicides of cyberbullied young people. The abuse extends to hate-filled and inflammatory comments appended to the online versions of newspaper articles—comments that hijack legitimate discussions of current events and discourage people from participating.

Anonymity also facilitates the posting of anti-Semitic, racist and homophobic content across the Web.

To be sure, there is value in someone being able to use the Internet without being identified. Online privacy is a major issue today. And in the United States, we have had a great tradition of anonymous political speech. Elsewhere, dissidents in oppressive regimes have felt free to speak up precisely because they believe (perhaps erroneously) that they cannot be identified.

This is not a matter for government, given the strictures of the First Amendment. But it is time for Internet intermediaries voluntarily to consider requiring either the use of real names (or registration with the online service) in circumstances, such as the comments section for news articles, where the benefits of anonymous posting are outweighed by the need for greater online civility.

There is no bright-line test, but Internet sites permitting user-generated postings can make a judgment that in some instances the use of real names benefits society.

CHRISTOPHER WOLF
Washington, Nov. 20, 2011

The writer is an Internet and privacy attorney and leads the Internet Task Force of the Anti-Defamation League.

READERS REACT

When striking down a law prohibiting anonymous distribution of leaflets, the Supreme Court wrote that anonymity serves "to protect unpopular individuals from retaliation—and their ideas from suppression—at the hand of an intolerant society."

It's no secret that some people use anonymity to say vile things about others. But before urging the likes of Facebook and Google to banish such speech, think about the gay person who isn't in a position to come out in the "real world," but feels comfortable doing so online. Those who need help with personal problems. Those with political opinions they don't want their bosses to hear.

Or think about your younger self, and whether you'd want everything you said as a teenager to be permanently linked to your real name.

Ugly insults are just one small part of all the free speech that anonymity makes possible, and it's not worth closing the door on all that speech to make the world more polite.

CATHERINE CRUMP
New York, Nov. 23, 2011

The writer is a lawyer with the American Civil Liberties Union.

In my years of active engagement as a commenter on various Web sites, I have consistently used my full name, which means that I try to say only what I truly believe, say it respectfully, and say only those things that I am willing to have permanently attached to my name.

That said, I think there should also be the option of anonymity, if not in registering on a site, at least in one's posting. There have been a few times when I have participated in a discussion of a topic that is personal or sensitive for me. In order to protect my own privacy and the privacy of family or friends, I have, in such discussions, used only part of my name or even just my location.

I have a rather easily identifiable name. To require that I use my full name at all times would be to silence me on some topics on which I have meaningful experience to contribute.

ANNE-MARIE HISLOP
Chicago, Nov. 21, 2011

My partners and I are the proprietors of The Robing Room (www.therobing-room.com), which permits lawyers and laypersons to post anonymous evaluations of judges in the federal and state courts. Without doubt our participation rate would fall precipitously if we insisted that posters identify themselves, and the public would lose the benefit of a frank, public forum to discuss the merits—and demerits—of sitting judges.

That said, we agree that a judge should not be left solely at the mercy of anonymous posters, and on occasion we remove inappropriate comments.

My partners and I are all for online civility, but we are not willing to sacrifice a robust public forum to achieve it.

RICHARD LEVITT
New York, Nov. 21, 2011

Mr. Wolf astutely observes that anonymity online can unlock people's rage. Why not vent bigotry, spread lies or threaten others if no one can identify us to hold us accountable?

Intermediaries' insistence that users employ their real names might stem the tide of incivility and hate online. But its costs may not outweigh its benefits. Without anonymity, victims of domestic violence and sexual assault might not join online survivors groups for fear that their abusers might discover them.

Lesbian, gay, bisexual and transgender teenagers might decline to seek advice about coping with bullying. Blogging may be less attractive to women; writing under female names raises one's risk of cyberharassment.

Rather than a mandatory real-name policy, intermediaries ought to adopt anonymity as their default setting, a privilege that can be lost by harming others in ways that intermediaries find unacceptable. That preserves anonymity's upside potential and potentially forestalls its downside.

DANIELLE KEATS CITRON
Baltimore, Nov. 21, 2011

The writer is a professor at the University of Maryland School of Law.

Mr. Wolf underestimates the risk that employees of many institutions would incur if they posted their opinions in public for attribution. A post need not be a flame or a troll to endanger someone's livelihood. I can't be the only person who would have to stop posting if I had to take ownership of everything I said.

It could be argued that I would not lose much if I censored myself. But there is a centuries-old tradition of using noms de plume when commenting on the issues of the day. I would like to see it stay that way. This comment, at least, I can claim.

JULIA HOLCOMB
Leesburg, Va., Nov. 21, 2011

There is an element of risk associated with attaching one's name to an individual opinion made public.

On the other hand, expressing an opinion lacking the element of risk is usually not worthwhile.

WILLIAM SCARBROUGH
Columbus, Ind., Nov. 21, 2011

My thoughtful friend Chris Wolf is correct that real-name policies on the Internet promote civility. But they also inhibit us from saying controversial things, which is why they are powerful. And dangerous.

Imagine a Facebook-style real-name policy applied to the whole Internet. Everything we said could be linked to us. Forever. On controversial topics, this can deter speech.

Real-name policies reduce some (but not most) offensive speech, but they also deter people from contributing thoughtfully to controversial topics. Many of the strongest arguments for anonymous speech were made by the N.A.A.C.P. and other dissidents in the 1950s and 1960s. Their political opponents wanted to obtain their names in order to retaliate against them. Sometimes anonymity allows us to speak the unpopular truth.

Anonymous speech can be abused, but it can be useful. And the bad can be impossible to separate from the good. It's like a lot of our other civil liberties in that respect.

NEIL M. RICHARDS
St. Louis, Nov. 21, 2011

The writer is a professor of law at Washington University.

Mr. Wolf undercuts his own argument against online anonymity very effectively. After stating, without proof, that real-name policies promote civility, he then cites America's great tradition of anonymous political speech, the benefits of anonymity for dissidents in oppressive regimes, and the First Amendment complications of enforcing any such policy all before concluding that the use of real names benefits society "in some instances."

It appears that Mr. Wolf disagrees with himself almost as much as I do.

TONY BOZANICH
New York, Nov. 21, 2011

Mr. Wolf states that "the benefits of anonymous posting are outweighed by the need for greater online civility." I strongly disagree.

Free expression is enhanced by anonymity. Unfortunately our society tends to vilify those who express a minority opinion. Atheists, homosexuals and others may well expect retaliation for expressing their views openly online. The ability to remain anonymous online offers minorities the protection they need to make themselves heard.

While I agree that cyber-bullying is a problem that must be addressed, a more appropriate response to overtly abusive online behavior is to have vigilant site managers.

Otherwise, the occasional lack of civility is a consequence of a robust tradition of free speech and should not be encumbered.

ANDRE M. GORELKIN
Roseland, N.J., Nov. 21, 2011

Mr. Wolf confirms what I have experienced all too often when he writes that allowing anonymous or pseudonymous names on Internet commentary sites leads to abusive "comments that hijack legitimate discussions of current events and discourage people from participating."

Both online and offline, not a day goes by without someone bemoaning the polarizing atmosphere that pollutes our political landscape. More than ever, we need to search out and interact with people who are not members of our own choir. The Internet provides a great resource for doing this.

What about encouraging Internet sites to have two sets of commentary—one would be anonymous, and the other would use real names. The use of real names would promote civility and genuine dialogue. The anonymous site would preserve the "great tradition of anonymous political speech."

That would give the reader a choice.

BILL SWEENEY
Shorewood, Wis., Nov. 21, 2011

THE WRITER RESPONDS

My proposal for Internet companies to consider, in appropriate circumstances, a real-name policy decidedly does not include a call for the end of anonymity on the Internet.

To be clear, I agree that free expression, which anonymity promotes, is a cherished value. I agree with several of the writers, including Ms. Hislop, Ms. Holcomb, Ms. Crump and Professor Citron, that real-name identification could lead to harassment of and retaliation against vulnerable people or those expressing unpopular positions, and free expression could be stifled. I understand why a gay teenager would want to communicate under a pseudonym to avoid being bullied at school.

But human dignity is also a cherished value. And uninhibited free expression online promoted by anonymity can result in an assault on human dignity in ways that pamphlets on street corners never could.

The anonymity enjoyed by the gay teenager as a shield can be used as a sword against people like him by online bullies and hate groups. Anonymity can indeed lead to harm. The online hacking group Anonymous, dedicated to committing harm, chose its name advisedly. Anonymity is not going away. So a balance can be struck between ensuring the opportunity to participate online for those whose rights will be advanced by anonymity and ensuring that free expression and human dignity are not hijacked by those hiding behind online anonymity, who intentionally want to hurt others and disrupt civil discourse.

Requiring commenters to use real names demonstrably promotes civil discourse, as does moderating comments, as some newspapers, like the *Times*, have demonstrated. And I like the idea of sites giving priority placement to those who use their real names.

Fundamentally, as someone fighting online hate, I wish that Internet companies would do more to police online hate speech and enforce their terms of service, and if they did so, there would be less need for a real-name policy.

CHRISTOPHER WOLF
Washington, Nov. 22, 2011

Appendix D

MYSPACE-RELATED SUICIDE PUTS FOCUS ON CYBER-BULLYING

From the PBS News Hour *that examines the legal and social implications of the use of the Internet as a weapon for bullying and harassment.*

From The NewsHour *with Jim Lehrer (May 16, 2008) © 2008 MacNeil/Lehrer Productions. Reprinted with Permission.*

A Missouri woman was indicted on federal charges related to the suicide of a 13-year-old MySpace user this week. An Internet and privacy lawyer considers the world of cyber-bullying and how the law and the use of the Web intersect.

JUDY WOODRUFF: Finally tonight, a Media Unit look at a case of online bullying. And once again to Jeffrey Brown.

TINA MEIER, Mother of Megan Meier: She deserves the life sentence that our family has been given, and 20 years is unfortunately not enough for her.

JEFFREY BROWN: That was the reaction of Tina Meier to news that a Missouri neighbor had been indicted in Los Angeles for cyber-bullying Meyer's daughter, Megan.

Megan hanged herself in 2006 after receiving an online message on her MySpace page, supposedly from a boy named Josh Evans, that, quote, "the world would be better off without her."

Investigators say "Josh" was really Lori Drew, the mother of a classmate and former friend of Megan's.

Drew, who has denied any involvement, now faces charges of conspiracy and computer fraud.

And with me to look at this case and the state of cyber law in this area is Christopher Wolf, an Internet and privacy attorney in private practice. He also chairs the International Network Against Cyberhate, a group based in Amsterdam that works against discrimination on the Internet.

Welcome to you.

CHRISTOPHER WOLF, Internet and Privacy Lawyer: Thank you, Jeff.

INITIALLY, DIFFICULT TO PROSECUTE

JEFFREY BROWN: Now, this case got a lot of attention when the suicide occurred, but it was not clear, if I remember right, that it would proceed to a legal matter. Is that because the state of the law is so unformed or new?

CHRISTOPHER WOLF: Well, everyone was justifiably outraged when they read about what Lori Drew did that resulted in the suicide of Megan Meier. It was a despicable thing to do.

The prosecutors in Missouri apparently looked at the facts, and they looked at the law, and they couldn't find a fit. There's such a thing in criminal law known as an outrage prosecution, where the public is demanding a prosecution and prosecutors move forward.

The Missouri prosecutors appeared to resist that, and that's why there wasn't a prosecution there. And the thing basically went to sleep, in terms of any kind of legal activity.

JEFFREY BROWN: Now, federal prosecutors step in from Los Angeles. Why? And what are they charging her with?

CHRISTOPHER WOLF: Well, as to why, I really can't tell you, because what they did is extremely unusual. They used a law called the Computer Fraud and Abuse Act, which was passed to deal with people hacking into computers to either steal information or cause mischief to the computer system.

And basically what they've said is that Lori Drew, by falsifying the identity of someone named Josh, to be able to join MySpace, by lying to MySpace in order to become a member, and then interact with Megan Meier, effectively hacked into a computer system, and that that kind of fraudulent activity is a federal crime, according to the prosecutors in Los Angeles.

JEFFREY BROWN: And that's even though the Missouri state prosecutors didn't want to go that route?

CHRISTOPHER WOLF: Well, that's right. This is not a prosecution for causing the death of Megan Meier. It's a prosecution for accessing a protected computer, which is a federal crime.

It's the first time that that statute has ever been used for anything close to this. And if you think about it, the repercussions are pretty stunning, because any time anybody reads the terms of service that prohibit a whole range of activity and does something in violation of the terms of service, according to this indictment, that would be a federal criminal offense.

INTERNET HATE NOT A PRIORITY

JEFFREY BROWN: So there's not a federal law against cyber-bullying, per se?
CHRISTOPHER WOLF: No.
JEFFREY BROWN: Is there even a legal definition of cyber-bullying?
CHRISTOPHER WOLF: Well, there is, and it's pretty easy to define. It's a constant and hate-filled attack on a person using the Internet or other means of electronic communication.

Twelve states now have added to their anti-bullying legislation the offense of cyber-bullying. And those states have instructed their school system that, when this happens, you must do something.

You must protect the child who's the victim of cyber-bullying, and you must have some punishment that is on the books in the school regulations, and you must have rules and regulations about appropriate use of Internet tools. More states should have that.

JEFFREY BROWN: Yes, that's what I'm wondering. You were telling me before we started that you've been doing this Internet law since the advent of the Internet.

CHRISTOPHER WOLF: Right.

JEFFREY BROWN: Now, anybody of a certain age or parents of kids of a certain age—and I'm in that category—where we know kids are using MySpace, Facebook, all these social networking, and you see what's going on, the law is slowly developing around that, I guess?

CHRISTOPHER WOLF: Well, it is. And it's time now for the law to address the subject of hate on the Internet.

The Anti-Defamation League has developed a model legislation for states to adopt, like the ones that have adopted the 12 statutes. And it's time for all 50 states to do that.

But the broader issue of hate on the Internet has really taken a back seat to things like spam and obscenity and child predation, all admittedly important topics, but hate on the Internet has sort of fallen off the priority list. And things like the Megan Meier case suggest that it's really time for it to come back into the national agenda.

JEFFREY BROWN: One would think that there are First Amendment issues involved, as well. I mean, who decides what can be said and how?

CHRISTOPHER WOLF: Well, that's right. And yesterday I actually testified on the Senate side before Senator Cardin and we talked about that.

This is not an area where the government should regulate speech. Our First Amendment has an important role to play.

But the Internet industry, working with educators and working with NGOs like the Anti-Defamation League, as well as the International Network Against Cyberhate, ought to work together to educate parents and kids and to work with school systems to help kids protect themselves, but also to teach them to be better citizens online.

KIDS SHOULD REPORT CYBER-BULLYING

JEFFREY BROWN: Well, what steps do you advise to parents and young people if they see this or if they're the target of it?

CHRISTOPHER WOLF: Well, if kids are the target of cyber-bullying, they should immediately report it to their parents, and their parents should immediately report it to the school, because it's typically being done by a schoolmate or a classmate, and sometimes it's even being done over the school's Internet system.

JEFFREY BROWN: Unlike this case that we started with.

CHRISTOPHER WOLF: This is a very unusual case, the Megan Meier case, but it really serves as a wake-up call, with respect to the problem of cyber-bullying.

JEFFREY BROWN: And are companies like MySpace and others, are they taking action or able to take action to kind of patrol what goes on?

CHRISTOPHER WOLF: Well, you know, they're certainly able to take action. And, in my view, they ought to be playing a more proactive role to protect kids and to work with parents.

Now, they have been working with the attorneys general to stop child predation, to stop adults lurking online, preying on children. The next issue they ought to tackle certainly ought to be cyber-bullying.

JEFFREY BROWN: And, briefly, just to come back to this case, you said this was a kind of creative use of the law in this case. There is a question about whether it will stand up and where this case goes next.

CHRISTOPHER WOLF: Well, that's right. In the legal blogosphere, most legal experts think that this is a case that will not likely result in a conviction.

JEFFREY BROWN: OK, Christopher Wolf, thank you very much.

CHRISTOPHER WOLF: Thank you for having me.

Appendix E

BULLYING/ CYBER-BULLYING PREVENTION LAW

Excerpts from the ADL Model Statute and Advocacy Kit

For the complete package of materials provided by ADL, visit the organization's website at http://www.adl.org/civil_rights/Anti -Bullying%20Law%20Toolkit_2009.pdf.

I. INTRODUCTION

Bullying and harassment in elementary and secondary educational settings is a continuing problem for school districts, parents, and students. The impact of bullying has been well documented—studies have shown that difficulty making friends, loneliness, low self-esteem, depression, poor academic achievement, truancy, and suicide are all associated with being bullied.

Bullying is often motivated by prejudice and hate, and some of the most serious cases are the result of bias based on the victim's personal characteristics, such as race, religion, national origin, gender identity, or sexual orientation. Whether bullying is related to identity-based group membership, or more universal characteristics such as appearance or social status, this form of social cruelty can produce devastating consequences for the targets—and the perpetrators of bullying—and may be a precursor to more destructive behavior.

Cyber-bullying, described as intentional harm inflicted through electronic media, is a growing problem that affects almost half of all U.S. teens. An increasing number of youth are misusing online technology—emailing, text messaging, chatting, and blogging—to bully, harass, and even incite violence against others. Targets of cyber-bullying may be subject to additional distress due to the pervasive and invasive nature of modern communication technology. Cyber-bullying messages can be circulated far and wide in an instant and are usually irrevocable; cyber-bullying is ubiquitous—there is no refuge and victimization can be relentless; and cyber-bullying is often anonymous and can rapidly swell as countless and unknown others join in on "the fun."

For years, governments, schools, and courts have been wrestling with how to deal with the issue of bullying and harassment in schools. A school's duty to maintain a safe learning environment for students must be balanced with a student's right to privacy and free speech. Particularly with the rise in cyber-bullying, schools are seeking ways to create a safe environment, and communities and legislatures are creating guidelines on the issue.

Over the past ten years, thirty-seven states have adopted legislation mandating schools implement anti-bullying statutes. Some statutes are general prohibitions on bullying while others are specific in their requirements. The Anti-Defamation League has prepared a Model Anti-Bullying Statute. The League's Model Statute combines the best elements of existing laws, along with refinements to ensure that this anti-bullying statute is comprehensive and constitutional. While some of the current thirty-seven state statutes may have all of the elements in ADL's model, most do not.

ADL is taking a strong lead in encouraging states to ensure their anti-bullying statutes are complete, effective, constitutional, and implemented. This Toolkit contains ADL's Model Anti-Bullying Statute, general talking points in support of anti-bullying legislation, a specific section-by-section description of our model policy, and examples of school Internet Acceptable Use Policies.

II. TALKING POINTS IN SUPPORT OF THE ADL MODEL STATUTE

- Throughout the country, many school administrators now are dealing with the issue of bullying, and particularly cyber-bullying, in their schools.
    - All students have the right to participate fully in the educational process, free from harassment and bullying. Anti-bullying policies should be in place *before* an incident occurs.
    - Some schools may have policies, but parents and students may not even know they exist, they may not be consistently enforced, or they may be overbroad and unconstitutional. To be effective, statutes should be comprehensive and create accountability.
    - Students learn by example, and so administrators should set a tone of civility and respect, and demonstrate their refusal to tolerate bullying and harassment.
    - A law gives schools the power to do something about a bullying problem.
    - Without a law, school districts may choose not to create anti-bullying policies, or may not actually enforce policies.
    - ADL's mission in fighting hate and prejudice does not end at the schoolhouse doors. We continue our work so all children feel truly protected, including students who are bullied because of their ancestry, color, disability, ethnicity, gender, gender identity or expression, national origin, religion, race, or sex. Further, over the past number of years, it has become clear that new technologies have enabled bullying to take a new and ubiquitous form in cyberspace, and so the time for action is ripe and necessary.

III. ELEMENTS OF A COMPREHENSIVE ANTI-BULLYING LAW

(1) Require each school district to adopt an anti-bullying policy.

- A requirement will let the parents, students, and concerned community members know that the issue is being taken seriously.
    - The bill should require that school districts work with parents, teachers, students, law enforcement, and other community stakeholders in the creation and implementation of the policy. The issue of bullying is a community issue and any response needs the support and buy-in of the entire community.

(2) A strong definition of intimidation, harassment, and bullying is necessary.

- The definition will notify school administrators, students, and teachers exactly what is unacceptable.
  - The definition should not be overbroad or vague—it must not punish constitutionally protected speech. The definition should be limited to areas in which the school administration has the authority to act.

(3) Enumerated characteristics must be included in any definition of bullying.

- Naming certain categories provides clear guidance to those who must apply the standard.
  - Naming the categories (particularly sexual orientation) will remove all doubt that Lesbian, Gay, Bisexual, and Transgender (LGBT) youth are included in the protections from bullying. A recent national survey of a representative group of students ages 13 to 18 found that students in schools with bullying or harassment policies inclusive of sexual orientation or gender identity are less likely to report a serious harassment problem at their schools.[1]
  - Inclusion of enumerated characteristics does not affect protection for all other students.
  - The U.S. Supreme Court has found that "enumerating" personal characteristics is the "essential device used to make the duty not to discriminate concrete and to provide guidance for those who must comply."[2]
  - According to a GLSEN report, students who attend schools with policies that enumerate categories report less bullying and harassment than students who do not.
  - Students from schools with inclusive policies reported that other students are harassed less because of their physical appearance (36% v. 52%), their sexual orientation (32% v. 43%), or their gender identity (26% v. 37%).[3]

(4) "Electronic communications" must be included in any definition of bullying.

- With increasing access to online technology, the Internet has become yet another vehicle to harass and bully. Cyber-bullying may be more harmful than traditional bullying because of the invasive and pervasive nature of the communication: Messages are circulated far and wide and there is no refuge—it is ubiquitous.
  - In a survey of 824 13- to 17-year-olds, 35% reported being targeted by at least one of the following forms of Internet harassment in the previous year: rude or nasty comments, rumors, and threatening or aggressive

messages. Eight percent reported frequent harassment (being targeted monthly or more often).[4] In a survey of middle school students from a large U.S. school district, students who reported being cyber-bullied said that the bully was most often someone from school (26.5%).[5]

(5) Off-campus cyber-bullying, which affects and interferes with a school's educational mission, must be covered by the Act.

- As a significant amount of cyber-bullying is created on computers, cell-phones, and other devices that are not owned by the school, or are not located on school property, but still affect the school environment and the welfare of the students, it is important to ensure that schools are given adequate legal framework to address the issue.
  - While courts nationwide are engaging in debates about balancing a student's right to free speech with another student's right to learn in a safe environment when dealing with electronic harassment, most courts agree that schools may discipline speech, which results in a substantial disruption of the operation of the school.

(6) In school reporting: A process within the school for reporting and investigating bullying must be established.

- Students and witnesses should know a safe place to come to report incidents.
  - There should be a point person in the school who is responsible for receiving reports of bullying and communicating with appropriate personnel for investigation.

(7) District Reporting: A systematic process by which the school reports to the school district, and the school district reports to the State, must be established.

- The bill should create a process for schools to report incidents to the superintendents, who must then report to the designated state repository agency.
  - State authorities must set an example that this is an important issue that is being monitored and examined.

(8) Establish consequences for unacceptable activity.

  - Establishing consequences is important to put students, and staff, on notice that inappropriate behavior will not be tolerated and will be taken seriously.

(9) Mandate training for faculty and students.

- Thorough training of school administrators, teachers, and counseling staff is essential to ensure that the Model Policy is properly implemented and enforced.

- A section such as this may have clear resource implications. It may be necessary for supporters to advocate for funds to accompany the enactment of this statute.

(10) Include counseling for victims and perpetrators.

- The bill should include a section on counseling for both targets and perpetrators, and for appropriate family members, affected by bullying. As described in the introduction above, severe bullying can have long-lasting and dangerous effects on students.

(11) Give notice to parents and guardians.

- This bill should ensure there is a procedure for broadly publicizing the policy (in conduct codes, handbooks, bulletin boards, school Web sites, and other appropriate places).
  - The notice will send a message to students, teachers, and parents that the school is taking this issue seriously and does not accept inappropriate conduct.
  - The notice will also serve to instruct students, parents, and school staff how to identify, respond to, and report incidents of bullying.

(12) The State Board of Education should play a significant role.

- The bill should require the Board of Education to create a Model Policy. School Districts will take their lead from the Superintendents and the State Department of Education. The State should lead by example and provide inclusive sample policies so that schools districts have guidance in creating comprehensive policies.

IV. ADL MODEL ANTI-BULLYING STATUTE

(A) Prohibited Activities:

(1) Harassment, Intimidation, Bullying, and Cyber-bullying, prohibited:

1. (a) No student shall be subjected to harassment, intimidation, bullying, or cyber-bullying in any public educational institution,

(i) During any education program or activity; or

(ii) While in school, on school equipment or property, in school vehicles, on school buses, at designated school bus stops, at school-sponsored activities, at school-sanctioned events; or

(iii) Through the use of data, telephone, or computer software that is accessed through a computer, computer system, or computer network of any public educational institution.

1. (b) As used in this Act, "harassment, intimidation, bullying or cyber-bullying" means any written, verbal, or physical act, or any electronic communication including, but not limited to, one shown to be motivated by a

student's actual or perceived race, color, religion, national origin, ancestry or ethnicity, sexual orientation, physical, mental, emotional, or learning disability, gender, gender identity and expression, or other distinguishing personal characteristic, or based on association with any person identified above, when the written, verbal or physical act or electronic communication is intended to:

(i) Physically harm a student or damage the student's property; or

(ii) Substantially interfere with a student's educational opportunities; or

(iii) Be so severe, persistent, or pervasive that it creates an intimidating or threatening educational environment; or

(iv) Substantially disrupt the orderly operation of the school.

1. (c) As used in this Section, "electronic communication" means any communication through an electronic device including but not limited to a telephone, cellular phone, computer, or pager, which communication includes but is not limited to E-Mail, instant messaging, text messages, blogs, mobile phones, pagers, online games, and Web sites.[6]

(B) School Board Requirements and Responsibilities

(1) Each school district shall adopt a policy prohibiting harassment, intimidation, bullying, and cyber-bullying, which includes the definition in this Act.

(2) The school district shall involve students, parents, administrators, school staff, school volunteers, community representatives, and local law enforcement agencies in the process of adopting the policy. The school district policy must be implemented in a manner that is ongoing throughout the school year and integrated with a school's curriculum, a school's discipline policies, and other violence prevention efforts.[7]

(3) The policy shall contain, at a minimum, the following components:

(a) Notice

(i) A statement prohibiting harassment, intimidation, bullying, or cyber-bullying of a student, as defined above;

(ii) A statement prohibiting retaliation or false accusation against a target, witness, or one with reliable information about an act of bullying, harassment, and intimidation;

(iii) A requirement that all students are protected regardless of their status under the law;

(iv) A statement of how the policy is to be publicized, including requirements that: annual written notice of the policy is provided to parents, guardians, staff, volunteers, and students, with age appropriate language for students; the policy is posted throughout all schools in the district, including but not limited to cafeterias, school bulletin boards, administration offices, and the school district's Web site; and the policy is included in all student and employee handbooks;

(v) A procedure for providing immediate notification to the parents or guardian of a victim of harassment, intimidation, bullying, or cyber-bullying and the parents or guardian of the perpetrator of the harassment, intimidation, bullying, or cyber-bullying;

(vi) The identification by job title of school officials responsible for ensuring that the policy is implemented.

(vii) A statement that this policy will apply to an electronic communication whether or not this conduct originated on school property or with school equipment so long as:

1. (1) a reasonable person should know, under the circumstances, that the act will have the effect of harming a student or damaging the student's property, or placing a student in reasonable fear of harm to his or her person or damage to his or her property; and has the effect of insulting or demeaning any student or group of students in such a way as to cause substantial disruption in, or substantial interference with, the orderly operation of the school; or

1. (2) the act is directed specifically at students and intended for the purpose of disrupting school, and has a high likelihood of succeeding in that purpose.[8]

2. (b) Reporting and Investigations

(i) A procedure for reporting an act of harassment, intimidation, bullying, or cyber-bullying, including a provision that permits a person to report such an act anonymously. No formal disciplinary action shall be taken solely on the basis of an anonymous report;

(ii) A requirement that any school employee that has reliable information that would lead a reasonable person to suspect that a person is a target of harassment, intimidation, bullying, or cyber-bullying shall immediately report it to the principal or the principal's designee;

(iii) A procedure for each school to document any prohibited incident that is reported and a procedure to report all incidents of harassment, intimidation, bullying, or cyber-bullying and the resulting consequences, including discipline and referrals, to the Board of Education on a semi-annual basis;

(iv) A procedure for reporting to law enforcement all acts of harassment, intimidation, bullying, or cyber-bullying which may constitute criminal activity;[9]

(v) A procedure for prompt investigation of reports of violations and complaints, identifying either the principal or the principal's designee as the person responsible for the investigation.

2. (c) Remedies and Victim Assistance

(i) Consequences and appropriate remedial action for a person who commits an act of harassment, intimidation, bullying, or cyber-bullying;

(ii) Consequences and appropriate remedial action for a student found to have falsely accused another as a means of retaliation, reprisal, or as a means of harassment, intimidation, bullying, or cyber-bullying;

(iii) A strategy for providing counseling or referral to appropriate services, including guidance, academic intervention, and protection to students, both targets and perpetrators, and appropriate family members, affected by harassment, intimidation, bullying, or cyber-bullying, as necessary;

(iv) A statement encouraging public schools and school districts to form bullying prevention task forces, programs, and other initiatives involving school staffs, pupils, administrators, volunteers, parents, law enforcement, community members, and other stakeholders.[10]

(4) Training and Assessment

Each school district shall provide the following educational programs in its efforts to prevent harassment, intimidation, bullying, or cyber-bullying:

(a) Annual training for administrators, school employees, and volunteers who have significant contact with students in preventing, identifying, responding to, and reporting incidents of harassment, intimidation, bullying, or cyber-bullying; and

(b) An educational program for students and parents in preventing, identifying, responding to, and reporting incidents of harassment, intimidation, bullying, or cyber-bullying.[11]

(C) State Board of Education Requirements and Responsibilities

The State Board of Education shall:

(1) Develop a model policy and training materials on the components that should be included in any district policy.

(2) Periodically review school district programs, activities, and services to determine whether the school boards are complying with this statute.

(3) Compile and make available to all schools a list of programs appropriate for the prevention of harassment, intimidation, bullying, or cyber-bullying of students.

(4) Establish and maintain a central repository for the collection and analysis of information regarding harassment, intimidation, bullying, or cyber-bullying as defined in this statute.

(5) Report to the state legislature annually on the current levels and nature of harassment, intimidation, and bullying in the schools and the effectiveness of school policies under this statute in combating harassment, intimidation, bullying, or cyber-bullying, including recommendations for appropriate actions to address identified problems.[12]

(D) Immunity

A school employee, school volunteer, student, parent, or guardian who promptly reports in good faith an act of harassment, intimidation, bullying, or cyber-bullying to the appropriate school official designated in the school district's policy and who makes this report in compliance with the procedures set forth in the policy is immune from a cause of action for damages arising out of the reporting itself or any failure to remedy the reported incident.[13]

(E) Qualification for Safe Schools Funding

(1) Distribution of safe schools funds to a school district is contingent upon the State Board of Education approval of the school district's anti-bullying policy. The Board's approval of each school district's anti-bullying policy

shall be granted upon certification by the Board that the school district's policy has been submitted to the Board and is in substantial conformity with the Board's model anti-bullying policy.

(2) Distribution of safe schools funds provided to a school district shall be contingent upon and payable to the school district upon the school district's compliance with all reporting procedures contained in this section.[14]

(F) Preclusion

(1) This act shall not be interpreted to prevent a target from seeking redress under any other available law either civil or criminal.

(2) Nothing in this statute is intended to infringe upon the right of a school employee or student to exercise their right of free speech.[15]

(G) Severability

If any provision of this act or the application thereof to any person or circumstance is held invalid, the invalidity shall not affect other provisions or applications of the act which can be given effect without the invalid provision or application, and to this end the provisions of this act are declared severable.[16]

V. MODEL SCHOOL INTERNET ACCEPTABLE USE POLICY

While this toolkit is focused on advocacy in state legislatures, it is also important to be able to make suggestions to schools about implementation. One important way to fulfill the "Notice" requirement to let students and parents know what is unacceptable behavior is to create a "School Internet Acceptable Use Policy" and insist that students and parents sign it.

A good Acceptable Use Policy (AUP) will encourage acceptable behavior by outlining the terms and conditions of Internet use. The Agreement should provide a written description of the consequences for wrongful action and set out the positive uses for the Internet in school.

We have included two resources that can be used when discussing this with schools:

(1) Education World(r), an online resource for educators, offers suggestions for educators developing a workable AUP for their schools.

(2) The Department of Justice Computer Crime & Intellectual Property Section has developed a model AUP for schools.

Education World's guidelines for an acceptable use policy appear below.

WHAT IS AN AUP?

The National Education Association (NEA) suggests that an effective AUP contain the following six key elements:

A preamble,

A definition section,
A policy statement,
An acceptable uses section,
An unacceptable uses section, and
A violations/sanctions section.

The **preamble** explains why the policy is needed, its goals, and the process of developing the policy. This section should say that the school's overall code of conduct also applies to student online activity.

The **definition section** defines key words used in the policy. Words and terms such as Internet, computer network, education purpose, and other possibly ambiguous terms need to be defined and explained to ensure student and parent comprehension.

A **policy statement** must tell what computer services are covered by the AUP and the circumstances under which students can use computer services. Schools may, for example, base student access to computer services on the completion of a "computer responsibility" class that will enhance student understanding of the AUP guidelines.

The **acceptable uses section** must define appropriate student use of the computer network. It may, for example, limit student use of the network to "educational purposes," which then must be defined.

In the **unacceptable uses section,** the AUP should give clear, specific examples of what constitutes unacceptable student use. In determining what is unacceptable, the committee charged with drafting the AUP must consider

- what kind of computer network sites, if any, should be off limits to students;
- what kind of student sending, forwarding, or posting of information, if any, should be prohibited; and
- what kind of student behavior will be destructive to the computer network services and should, therefore, be restricted.

Among the sites that might be off limits to students are chat rooms and term paper vendors. In addition, AUPs often prohibit students from sending, forwarding, or posting sexually explicit messages, profanity, and harassing or violent messages.

The **violations/sanctions section** should tell students how to report violations of the policy or whom to question about its application. "As a practical matter," says the NEA, "the AUP may simply provide that violations will be handled in accordance with the school's general student disciplinary code."

MODEL ACCEPTABLE USE POLICY INFORMATION TECHNOLOGY RESOURCES IN THE SCHOOLS

Adapted from the U.S. Department of Justice (www.cybercrime.gov)

The school's information technology resources, including email and Internet access, are provided for educational purposes. Adherence to the following policy is necessary for continued access to the school's technological resources:

Students must

1. Respect and protect the privacy of others.

- Use only assigned accounts.
- Not view, use, or copy passwords, data, or networks to which they are not authorized.
- Not distribute private information about others or themselves.

2. Respect and protect the integrity, availability, and security of all electronic resources.

- Observe all network security practices, as posted.
- Report security risks or violations to a teacher or network administrator.
- Not destroy or damage data, networks, or other resources that do not belong to them, without clear permission of the owner.
- Conserve, protect, and share these resources with other students and Internet users.

3. Respect and protect the intellectual property of others.

- Not infringe copyrights (no making illegal copies of music, games, or movies!).
- Not plagiarize.

4. Respect and practice the principles of community.

- Communicate only in ways that are kind and respectful.
- Report threatening or discomforting materials to a teacher.
- Not intentionally access, transmit, copy, or create material that violates the school's code of conduct (such as messages that are pornographic, threatening, rude, discriminatory, or meant to harass).
- Not intentionally access, transmit, copy, or create material that is illegal (such as obscenity, stolen materials, or illegal copies of copyrighted works).
- Not use the resources to further other acts that are criminal or violate the school's code of conduct.
- Not send spam, chain letters, or other mass unsolicited mailings.
- Not buy, sell, advertise, or otherwise conduct business, unless approved as a school project.

Students may, if in accord with the policy above

1. Design and post webpages and other material from school resources.

2. Use direct communications such as IRC, online chat, or instant messaging with a teacher's permission.

3. Install or download software, if also in conformity with laws and licenses, and under the supervision of a teacher.

4. Use the resources for any educational purpose.

Consequences for Violation. Violations of these rules may result in disciplinary action, including the loss of a student's privileges to use the school's information technology resources.

Supervision and Monitoring. School and network administrators and their authorized employees monitor the use of information technology resources to help ensure that uses are secure and in conformity with this policy. Administrators reserve the right to examine, use, and disclose any data found on the school's information networks in order to further the health, safety, discipline, or security of any student or other person, or to protect property. They may also use this information in disciplinary actions, and will furnish evidence of crime to law enforcement.

I ACKNOWLEDGE AND UNDERSTAND MY OBLIGATIONS:

_____ Student/Date

_____ Parent/Guardian Date

PARENTS, PLEASE DISCUSS THESE RULES WITH YOUR STUDENT TO ENSURE HE OR SHE UNDERSTANDS THEM.

THESE RULES ALSO PROVIDE A GOOD FRAMEWORK FOR YOUR STUDENT'S USE OF COMPUTERS AT HOME, AT LIBRARIES, OR ANYWHERE.

Appendix F

EXCERPTS FROM HATE CRIMES LAWS— THE ADL APPROACH

To see the entire package of materials on hate crimes laws provided by ADL, visit the organization's website at http://www.adl.org /99hatecrime/intro.asp.

I. INTRODUCTION

All Americans have a stake in an effective response to violent bigotry. Hate crimes demand a priority response because of their special emotional and psychological impact on the victim and the victim's community. The damage done by hate crimes cannot be measured solely in terms of physical injury or dollars and cents. Hate crimes may effectively intimidate other members of the victim's community, leaving them feeling isolated, vulnerable, and unprotected by the law. By making members of minority communities fearful, angry, and suspicious of other groups—and of the power structure that is supposed to protect them—these incidents can damage the fabric of our society and fragment communities.

ADL has long been in the forefront of national and state efforts to deter and counteract hate-motivated criminal activity. Hate crime statutes are necessary because the failure to recognize and effectively address this unique type of crime could cause an isolated incident to explode into widespread community tension.

In June 1993, the U.S. Supreme Court upheld a Wisconsin hate crime statute that was based on model legislation originally drafted by the Anti-Defamation League (ADL) in 1981 (*Wisconsin v. Mitchell*, 508 U.S. 476 [1993]).

The following year, ADL published a detailed report on hate crimes laws, "Hate Crimes Laws: A Comprehensive Guide," which functions as a reference on hate crimes legislation nationwide. This update is meant to complement the 1994 report and encompasses changes that have occurred since that time, including the League's recent addition of gender to its model hate crimes legislation, the passage of additional Federal legislation, as well as a description of a number of federal training and education initiatives to confront hate violence.

ADL MODEL LEGISLATION

The ADL model hate crimes legislation has been drafted to cover not just anti-Semitic crimes, but all hate crimes. Currently, 43 states and the District of Columbia have enacted laws similar to or based on the ADL model, and almost every state has some form of legislation that can be invoked to redress bias-motivated crimes.

The core of the ADL legal approach is a "penalty-enhancement" concept. In a landmark decision issued in June 1993, the U.S. Supreme Court unanimously upheld the constitutionality of Wisconsin's penalty-enhancement hate crimes statute, which was based on the ADL model. Expressions of hate protected by the First Amendment's free speech clause are not criminalized. However, criminal activity motivated by hate is subject to a stiffer sentence. A defendant's sentence may be enhanced if he intentionally selects his victim based upon his perception of the victim's race, religion, national origin, sexual orientation, or gender.[1]

The ADL model statute also includes an institutional vandalism section that increases the criminal penalties for vandalism aimed at houses of worship, cemeteries, schools, and community centers. This provision is useful in dealing with crimes such as the very disturbing series of arsons that have occurred at black churches across the South in recent years. The legislation also creates a civil action for victims and provides for other additional forms of relief, including recovery of punitive damages and attorney's fees and parental liability for minor children's actions. Finally, the model legislation includes a section on bias crime reporting and training, since accurate, comprehensive data are essential in combating hate crimes.

THE INCLUSION OF GENDER

In 1996, the ADL added gender to its model hate crimes legislation. The League chose to add gender after coming to the determination that gender-based hate crimes could not be easily distinguished from other forms of hate-motivated violence. Gender-based crimes, like other hate crimes, have a special psychological and emotional impact that extends beyond the original victim. The inclusion of gender is important because it sends the message that gender-based crimes will not be tolerated.

In the past eight years, as state legislators have realized that it is difficult to distinguish race-based and religion-based hate crimes from gender-based hate crimes, the trend has been to include gender in hate crimes legislation. In 1990, only seven of the 31 states that had hate crime statutes included gender. Today, 19 of the 41 statutes cover victims chosen by reason of their gender. Furthermore, the Federal Violence Against Women Act of 1994 (VAWA) allows individuals to file federal civil law suits in cases of gender-based violence. (See Section V(C) below.)

After studying the statutes in which gender is included, ADL came to the conclusion that the inclusion of gender has not overwhelmed the reporting system, nor has it distracted the criminal justice system from vigorous action against traditional hate-based crimes. Clearly not all crimes against women are gender-based crimes, and prosecutors have discretion in identifying those crimes that should be prosecuted as hate crimes. Prosecutors also must have concrete admissible evidence of bias to charge an individual with commission of a hate crime. Even in cases where gender bias can be proven, prosecutors may decide that the penalty imposed by the underlying crime is in itself sufficient and penalty enhancement is therefore unnecessary. It is also important to realize that there has not been an overwhelming number of gender-based crimes reported as an extension of domestic violence and rape cases.

TEXT OF ADL MODEL LEGISLATION

1. Institutional Vandalism

A. A person commits the crime of institutional vandalism by knowingly vandalizing, defacing, or otherwise damaging:
   i. Any church, synagogue, or other building, structure, or place used for religious worship or other religious purpose;
   ii. Any cemetery, mortuary, or other facility used for the purpose of burial or memorializing the dead;
   iii. Any school, educational facility, or community center;
   iv. The grounds adjacent to, and owned or rented by, any institution, facility, building, structure, or place described in subsections (i), (ii), or (iii) above; or
   v. Any personal property contained in any institution, facility, building, structure, or place described in subsections (i), (ii), or (iii) above.
B. Institutional vandalism is punishable as follows:
   i. Institutional vandalism is a _____ misdemeanor if the person does any act described in subsection A that causes damage to, or loss of, the property of another.
   ii. Institutional vandalism is a _____ felony if the person does any act described in Subsection A that causes damage to, or loss of, the property of another in an amount in excess of five hundred dollars.
   iii. Institutional vandalism is a _____ felony if the person does any act described in Subsection A that causes damage to, or loss of, the property of another in an amount in excess of one thousand five hundred dollars.
   iv. Institutional vandalism is a _____ felony if the person does any act described in Subsection A that causes damage to, or loss of, the property of another in an amount in excess of five thousand dollars.
C. In determining the amount of damage to, or loss of, property, damage includes the cost of repair or replacement of the property that was damaged or lost.

2. Bias-Motivated Crimes

A. A person commits a bias-motivated crime if, by reason of the actual or perceived race, color, religion, national origin, sexual orientation, or gender of another individual or group of individuals, he violates Section _____ of the Penal code (insert code provisions for criminal trespass, criminal mischief, harassment, menacing, intimidation, assault, battery, and/or other appropriate statutorily proscribed criminal conduct).

B. A bias-motivated crime under this code provision is a _____ misdemeanor/felony (the degree of criminal liability should be at least one degree more serious than that imposed for commission of the underlying offense).

3. Civil Action for Institutional Vandalism and Bias-Motivated Crimes

A. Irrespective of any criminal prosecution or result thereof, any person incurring injury to his person or damage or loss to his property as a result of conduct in violation of Sections 1 or 2 of this Act shall have a civil action to secure an injunction, damages, or other appropriate relief in law or in equity against any and all persons who have violated Sections 1 or 2 of this Act.

B. In any such action, whether a violation of Sections 1 or 2 of this Act has occurred shall be determined according to the burden of proof used in other civil actions for similar relief.

C. Upon prevailing in such civil action, the plaintiff may recover:
  i. Both special and general damages, including damages for emotional distress;
  ii. Punitive damages; and/or
  iii. Reasonable attorney fees and costs.

D. Notwithstanding any other provision of the law to the contrary, the parent(s) or legal guardian(s) of any unemancipated minor shall be liable for any judgment rendered against such minor under this Section.

4. Bias Crime Reporting and Training

A. The state police or other appropriate state law enforcement agency shall establish and maintain a central repository for the collection and analysis of information regarding Bias-Motivated Crimes as defined in Section 2. Upon establishing such a repository, the state police shall develop a procedure to monitor, record, classify, and analyze information relating to crimes apparently directed against individuals or groups, or their property, by reason of their actual or perceived race, color, religion, national origin, sexual orientation, or gender. The state police shall submit its procedure to the appropriate committee of the state legislature for approval.

B. All local law enforcement agencies shall report monthly to the state police concerning such offenses in such form and in such manner as prescribed by rules and regulations adopted by state police. The state police must summarize and analyze the information received and file an annual report with the governor and the appropriate committee of the state legislature.

C. Any information, records, and statistics collected in accordance with this subsection shall be available for use by any local law enforcement agency, unit of local government, or state agency, to the extent that such information is reasonably necessary or useful to such agency in carrying out the duties imposed upon it by law. Dissemination of such information shall be subject to all confidentiality requirements otherwise imposed by law.

The state police shall provide training for police officers in identifying, responding to, and reporting all bias-motivated crimes.

NOTES

CHAPTER 1: HATE DOESN'T JUST HURT—IT KILLS

1. Details on extremist organizations drawn from "Extremism in America: ADL's Guide," Anti-Defamation League, http://www.adl.org/main_Extremism/default .htm; and "Intelligence Files," Southern Poverty Law Center, http://www.splcen ter.org/get-informed/intelligence-files.

2. Andrew Backover, "Hate Sets up Shop on Internet," *Denver Post*, November 8, 1999, E-01.

3. Jessie Daniels, "Race, Civil Rights, and Hate Speech in the Digital Era," in *Learning Race and Ethnicity: Youth and Digital Media*, ed. Anna Everett, The John D. and Catherine T. MacArthur Foundation Series on Digital Media and Learning (Cambridge, MA: The MIT Press, 2008), 129-154.

4. Eric Lichblau, "Neo-Nazi Must Pay $1.1 Million to Fair Housing Activist," *Los Angeles Times*, July 21, 2000, http://articles.latimes.com/2000/jul/21/news/mn -56751; David Kohn, "Hate Hits Home," CBS News, February 11, 2009, http:// www.cbsnews.com/8301-18559_162-20759.html.

5. Jessie Daniels, "Searching for Dr. King: Teens, Race and Cloaked Websites," http:// hastac.org/informationyear/ET/BreakoutSessions/6/Daniels.

6. Leslie Meredith, "Obama Hate Speech Spreads on Facebook," *TechNewsDaily*, July 19, 2012, http://www.technewsdaily.com/4584-obama-hate-speech-spreads -on-facebook.html.

7. Lizzy Davies, "Facebook Refuses to Take Down Rape Joke Pages," *The Guardian*, September 30, 2011, http://www.guardian.co.uk/technology/2011/sep/30 /facebook-refuses-pull-rape-jokepages?newsfeed=true.

8. Lloyd Grove, "Facebook's Holocaust Problem," *The Daily Beast*, August 18, 2011, http://www.thedailybeast.com/articles/2011/08/18/facebook-s-holocaust -denial-hate-speech-problem.html.

9. Dodai Stewart, "Lowe's Facebook Page Explodes With Bigoted Hate Speech," *Jezebel*, December 14, 2011, http://jezebel.com/5867980/lowes-facebook-page -explodes-with-bigoted-hate-speech.

10. Nicholas K. Geraniols, "Hate Speech Corrodes Online Games," Associated Press, April 15, 2010, http://www.msnbc.msn.com/id/36572021/ns/technology_and _science-games/t/hate-speech-corrodes-online-games/#.UJkWFo6xGGk.

11. Susan Benesch, "Words as Weapons," *World Policy Journal*, spring 2012, http:// www.worldpolicy.org/journal/spring1012/words-weapons.

12. Profile of Gary "Gerhard" Lauck, *Intelligence Files*, Southern Poverty Law Center, http://www.splcenter.org/get-informed/intelligence-files/profiles/gary-gerhard-lauck.

13. Brian Levin, "Hate International," *Intelligence Report*, winter 2003, Southern Poverty Law Center, http://www.splcenter.org/get-informed/intelligence-report/browse-all-issues/2003/winter/hate-international.

14. http://www.thejc.com/news/uk-news/48825/race-hate-website-mans-jail-release.

15. Daniels, "Race, Civil Rights, and Hate Speech in the Digital Era."

16. Maria Papadopoulos, "Trial of Accused Murderer Keith Luke Set for October," *Enterprise News* [Brockton, MA], July 26, 2012, http://www.enterprisenews.com/topstories/x780624537/Trial-of-accused-murderer-Keith-Luke-set-for-October; Larry Keller, "Experts Discuss the Role of Race Propaganda after White Massachusetts Man Kills Two African Immigrants," *Intelligence Report*, summer 2009, Southern Poverty Law Center, http://www.splcenter.org/get-informed/intelligence-report/browse-all-issues/2009/summer/from-hate-to-hurt.

17. *iReport: Online Terror + Hate: The First Decade*, Simon Wiesenthal Center, http://www.wiesenthal.com/atf/cf/%7BDFD2AAC1-2ADE-428A-9263-352342 29D8D8%7D/IREPORT.PDF, page 8.

18. Gabriel Weimann, "How Modern Terrorism Uses the Internet," *The Journal of International Security Affairs*, spring 2005, http://www.securityaffairs.org/issues/2005/08/weimann.php.

19. Keller, "Experts Discuss the Role of Race Propaganda."

20. Ibid.

21. Ibid.

22. *Ten Ways To Fight Hate: A Community Response Guide*, 4th ed. (Montgomery, AL: Southern Poverty Law Center, 2010), http://cdna.splcenter.org/sites/default/files/downloads/publication/Ten_Ways_2010.pdf.

CHAPTER 2: WHAT IS INTERNET HATE?

1. Rachel Whetstone, "Our Approach to Free Expression and Controversial Content," *Official Google Blog*, March 20, 2012, http://googleblog.blogspot.com/2012/03/our-approach-to-free-expression-and.html.

2. Quoted in Rebecca J. Rosen, "What to Make of Google's Decision to Block the 'Innocence of Muslims' Movie," *The Atlantic*, September 14, 2012, http://www.theatlantic.com/technology/archive/2012/09/what-to-make-of-googles-decision-to-block-the-innocence-of-muslims-movie/262395/.

3. Ibid.

4. Sarah Chayes, "Does 'Innocence of Muslims' meet the free-speech test?" *Los Angeles Times*, September 18, 2012.

5. Interview with editor and researcher Karl Weber, October 5, 2012.

6. Erica Goode and Serge F. Kovaleski, "Wisconsin Killer Fed and Was Fueled by Hate-Driven Music," *New York Times*, August 6, 2012.

7. Ibid.

CHAPTER 3: "THERE OUGHTA BE A LAW"

1. See "Interview with Robert Post," in *The Content and Context of Hate Speech: Rethinking Regulation and Responses*, ed. Michael Herz and Peter Molnar (Cambridge, UK: Cambridge University Press, 2012), 11-13.

2. *Nat'l Socialist Party v. Village of Skokie,* 432 U.S. 43, 44 (1977).
3. *U.S. v. Watts,* 394 U.S. 707 (1969); *R.A.V. v. St. Paul,* 505 U.S. 377 (1992).
4. See, e.g., *United States v. Fulmer,* 108 F.3d 1486, 1491 (1st Cir. 1997); *United States v. Xiang Li,* 537 F. Supp 2d 431 (NDNY 2008).
5. 2009 U.S. App. LEXIS 15567, 2-5 (3d Cir. July 15, 2009).
6. *Brandenburg v. Ohio,* 395 U.S. 444, 447 (1969); see also *Hess v. Indiana,* 414 U.S. 105 (1973) (overturning disorderly conduct conviction of anti-war protestor who yelled "We'll take the f—ing street later (or again)"); *NAACP v. Claiborne Hardware Co.,* 458 U.S. 886 (1982).
7. 23 F. Supp. 2d 1182 (D. Or. 1999); 41 F. Supp. 2d 1130 (D. Or. 1999) (vacated and remanded); 244 F.3d 1007 (9th Cir. 2001) (reh'd en banc granted); 268 F.3d 908 (9th Cir. 2001) (affirmed in part, vacated in part and remanded); 290 F.3d 1058 (9th Cir. 2002).
8. Anti-Defamation League, *Jihad Online: Islamic Terrorists and the Internet* (2002), http://www.adl.org/internet/jihad.asp, 10-12.
9. Maureen O'Hagan, "A Terrorism Case That Went Awry," *Seattle Times,* November 22, 2004, http://seattletimes.com/html/localnews/2002097570_sami22m.html.
10. Joseph Brean, "Scrutinizing the Human Rights Machine: Commissions' Challenger Has Unlikely Allies," *National Post,* March 22, 2008.
11. Jeremy Waldron, *The Harm in Hate Speech* (Cambridge, MA: Harvard University Press, 2012), 41.
12. Ibid., 47.
13. Jamal Greene, "Hate Speech and the Demos," in *The Content and Context of Hate Speech: Rethinking Regulation and Responses,* ed. Michael Herz and Peter Molnar (Cambridge, UK: Cambridge University Press, 2012), 105.
14. "The Futility of Banning Hate Speech," *Wall Street Journal,* September 21, 2012, http://online.wsj.com/article/SB10000872396390443168045780038204461343 86.html.
15. Greene, "Hate Speech and the Demos," 97.
16. Michael Moynihan, "What the Islamists Get Right," *Tablet,* October 15, 2012.
17. Waldron, *The Harm in Hate Speech,* 99.

CHAPTER 4: HATE SPEECH AND THE GATEKEEPERS OF THE INTERNET

1. "Internet Usage Statistics," Internet World Stats, June 30, 2012, http://www.inter networldstats.com/stats.htm.
2. "The Size of the World Wide Web (The Internet)," WorldWideWebSize.com, accessed November 15, 2012, http://www.worldwidewebsize.com/.
3. "Hate on Display: A Visual Database of Racist Symbols, Logos, and Tattoos," Anti-Defamation League website, http://www.adl.org/hate_symbols/default.asp.
4. Basic ISP DSL Broadband End User Terms of Service Agreement, October 28, 2008, accessed November 15, 2012, http://www.basicisp.net/TOS/DSLTOS.aspx.
5. Frederick Lardinois, "ComScore: Google's Search Engine Market Share Increased in September," TechCrunch.com, October 11, 2012, http://techcrunch .com/2012/10/11/comscore-googles-search-engine-market-share-increased-in -september-yahoo-down-another-0-6-percentage-points/.
6. http://www.jewwatch.com/, accessed November 12, 2012.
7. Google explanation of search results, accessed November 15, 2012.
8. "Do We Need a Ministry of Truth for the Internet?" *Forbes,* January 29, 2012, http://www.forbes.com/sites/adamthierer/2012/01/29/do-we-need-a-ministry -of-truth-for-the-internet/2/.

9. "YouTube Community Guidelines," accessed October 18, 2012, http://www.you tube.com/t/community_guidelines.

10. "Facebook Blasted for Jewish Memes Page," JewishJournal.com, September 27, 2012, http://www.jewishjournal.com/culture/article/facebook_blasted_for _jewish_memes_page.

11. Quoted by Tzippe Barrow, "Facebook Closes 'Third Palestinian Intifada' Page," CBN News, March 29, 2011, http://www.cbn.com/cbnnews/insideisrael/2011 /march/facebook-third-palestinian-intifada-stays1/.

12. Quoted by Kevin Flower, "Facebook Page Supporting Palestinian Intifada Pulled Down," CNN News, March 29, 2011, http://articles.cnn.com/2011-03-29/world /palestinian.facebook_1_facebook-page-social-media-website-incites-violence? _s=PM:WORLD.

13. http://www.facebook.com/help/292517374180078/, accessed January 4, 2013.

14. Chloe Albanesius, "Facebook Estimates Put Fake, Questionable Accounts at 83 Million," PCMag.com, August 12, 2012, http://www.pcmag.com/arti cle2/0,2817,2407990,00.asp.

15. Michael Marshall, "Don't Flame Me, Bro'," *New Scientist* Technology blog, November 19, 2007, http://www.newscientist.com/blog/technology/2007/11/dont -flame-me-bro.html.

16. Somini Sengupta, "Rushdie Runs Afoul of Web's Real-Name Police," *New York Times,* November 14, 2011.

17. 357 U.S. 449 (1958).

18. 514 U.S. 334 (1995).

19. Danielle Keats Citron and Helen Norton, "Intermediaries and Hate Speech: Fostering Digital Citizenship for Our Information Age," *Boston University Law Review* 91 (2011): 1435-1484.

20. Lori Andrews, *I Know Who You Are and I Saw What You Did* (New York: Free Press, 2012).

21. Tim Wu, "When Censorship Makes Sense: How YouTube Should Police Hate Speech," *New Republic,* September 18, 2012.

CHAPTER 5: WHEN GOOD MEN DO NOTHING

1. William Saletan, "Muslims for Free Speech," *Slate,* October 3, 2012.

2. Halie Williams, "Social Media Exposes Internet Hate Speech at Ohio State," *The Lantern,* August 31, 2012, http://www.thelantern.com/campus/social-media -exposes-internet-hate-speech-at-ohio-state-1.2889977#.UH_3bY6xGGl.

3. Theresa Howard, "Online Hate Speech: Difficult to Police . . . and Define," *USA Today,* October 2, 2009.

4. Kevin O'Neil, "Wipeout Homophobia On Facebook: A Page With A Mission," Addicting Information website, October 18, 2011, http://www.addictinginfo .org/2011/10/18/wipeout-homohpobia-on-facebook-a-page-with-a-mission/.

5. "Hate Mail Replies," Wipeout Homophobia website, http://www.wipeouthomo phobia.com/hatemailreplies.htm.

6. Like all social networking sites, Facebook is subject to continual updating and revision. The description provided here is accurate as of November 2012.

7. "Interview with Kenan Malik," in *The Content and Context of Hate Speech: Rethinking Regulation and Responses,* ed. Michael Herz and Peter Molnar (Cambridge, UK: Cambridge University Press, 2012), 90-91.

8. Southern Poverty Law Center, *Ten Ways To Fight Hate: A Community Response Guide,* 4th ed. (Montgomery, AL: Southern Poverty Law Center, 2010), http://

cdna.splcenter.org/sites/default/files/downloads/publication/Ten_Ways_2010 .pdf, pages 7, 9, and 12.

CHAPTER 6: "YOU'VE GOT TO BE CAREFULLY TAUGHT"

1. Amy Gutmann, *Democratic Education* (Princeton, NJ: Princeton University Press, 1999), 52.
2. Jeffrey R. Young, "How to Combat a Campus Gossip Web Site (and Why You Shouldn't)," *Chronicle of Higher Education,* March 17, 2008, http://chronicle .com/article/How-to-Combat-a-Campus-Gossip/14266.
3. Andrew Born, "JuicyCampus," Case Studies in Ethics, The Kenan Institute for Ethics at Duke University, http://kenan.ethics.duke.edu/wp-content/up loads/2012/07/Case-Study-JuicyCampus.pdf, 4.
4. Ibid., 7.
5. "JuicyCampus Shuts Down, Kills the College Grapevine," *Los Angeles Times Technology,* February 4, 2009, http://latimesblogs.latimes.com/technology/2009/02 /juicy-campus.html.
6. Matt Ivester, *lol . . . OMG!—What Every Student Needs to Know About Online Reputation Management, Digital Citizenship and Cyberbullying,* http://www .lolomgbook.com/.
7. John A. Byrne, "From Gossip Site Founder to Web Reputation Defender," CNNMoney, October 12, 2011, http://management.fortune.cnn.com/2011/10 /12/from-gossip-site-founder-to-web-reputation-defender/.
8. Jessie Daniels, "Race, Civil Rights, and Hate Speech in the Digital Era," in *Learning Race and Ethnicity: Youth and Digital Media,* ed. Anna Everett, The John D. and Catherine T. MacArthur Foundation Series on Digital Media and Learning (Cambridge, MA: The MIT Press, 2008), 129-154.
9. Media Awareness Network, *Responding to Online Hate,* 2012, http://mediasmarts .ca/sites/default/files/pdfs/Responding_Online_Hate_Guide.pdf.
10. Jessie Daniels, *Cyber Racism: White Supremacy Online and the New Attack on Civil Rights* (Lanham, MD: Rowman & Littlefield, 2009).
11. Jessie Daniels, "Searching for Dr. King: Teens, Race and Cloaked Websites," http:// hastac.org/informationyear/ET/BreakoutSessions/6/Daniels.
12. Cited in Susan Dominus, "Underage on Facebook," *Redbook,* http://www.red bookmag.com/kids-family/advice/kids-on-facebook.
13. Lee Warren, "Managing Hot Moments in the Classroom," Derek Bok Center for Teaching and Learning, Harvard University, http://isites.harvard.edu/fs/html /icb.topic58474/hotmoments.html, 1-2.
14. "Interview with Robert Post," in *The Content and Context of Hate Speech: Rethinking Regulation and Responses,* ed. Michael Herz and Peter Molnar (Cambridge, UK: Cambridge University Press, 2012), 33.

APPENDIX E: BULLYING/CYBER-BULLYING PREVENTION LAW

1. *From Teasing to Torment: School Climate in America,* Dana Markow, Ph.D., GLSEN and Harris Interactive, Inc. (2005).
2. *Romer v. Evans,* 517 U.S. 620 (1996).
3. Ibid.
4. Michele L. Ybarra, Marie Diener-West, and Philip J. Leaf, 2007, "Examining the Overlap in Internet Harassment and School Bullying: Implications for School Intervention," *Journal of Adolescent Health* 41 (2007): S42-S50.

5. S. Hinduja and J. W. Patchin, *Bullying Beyond the Schoolyard: Preventing and Responding to Cyberbullying* (Thousand Oaks, CA: Sage Publications [Corwin Press], 2008).

6. Source: (A)(1)(a) adapted from FS 1006.147; A.C.A. § 6-18-514; AZ.R.S. Ann. § 15-341 (A)(1)(b) adapted from WA St. 28A.300.285; NJ 18A 37-14; Iowa Code Ann. § 280.28 (A)(1)(c) adapted from MD. Ann. Ed § 7-424.

7. Source: (B)(2) FS 1006.147.

8. Source: (B)(3)(a)(i) ORS §339.356(2)(a)-(b); (B)(3)(a)(ii) Alaska Stat. § 14.33.200-250 (B)(3)(a)(iii) Utah Code 53A-11a; (B)(3)(a)(vi) adapted from A.C.A. § 6-18-514; FLS § 1006.147; (B)(3)(a)(v) FLS § 1006.147; (B)(3)(a)(vi) ORS §339.362; (B)(3)(a)(viii) adapted from A.C.A. § 6-18-514(b)(2) and NJ St 18A:37-14(2).

9. Source: (B)(3)(b)(i) NJ St 18A:37-15(b)(5); (B)(3)(b)(ii) A.C.A. § 6-18-514(b) (4); (B)(3 (b)(iii) WV ST 18-2C-3(b)(6); Kentucky Acts Chap. 125; (B)(3)(b)(iv) Utah Code 53A-11a.

10. Source: (B)(3)(c)(i) NJ St 18A:37-15(b)(4); (B)(3)(c)(ii) NJ St 18A:37-15(b) (9); (B)(3)(c)(iii) adapted from FLS § 1006.147; (B)(3)(c)(iv) R.I. Gen. Laws § 16-21-26.

11. Source: (B)(4)(a) adapted from NJ ST 18A:37-17(b)-(c) and FLS § 1006.147; (B) (4)(b) adapted from MD. Ann. Ed § 7-424.

12. Source: (C)(1) adapted from A.C.A. § 6-18-514(e); (C)(2) Wash. Rev. Code 28A.300.285(4); (C)(3) OK St. § 70-24-100.2-5; (C)(4) adapted from Kentucky Acts Chap. 125; (C)(5) adapted from MD. Ann. Ed § 7-424.

13. Source: (D) adapted from A.C.A. § 6-18-514(b)(2) and NJ St 18A:37-14(2).

14. Source: (E) adapted from FS 1006.147 and 14 Del. Code Ann. § 4112D.

15. Source: (F)(1) NJ ST 18A:37-18; (F)(2) Utah Code 53A-11a-301(6).

16. Source: (G) FS 1006.147.

APPENDIX F: EXCERPTS FROM HATE CRIMES LAWS—THE ADL APPROACH

1. The ADL model statute arguably also covers crimes committed against persons who are associated with the targeted group. For example, the statute would cover crimes committed against either or both members of a mixed-race couple if it can be demonstrated that the crimes occurred because of one's race. *In Illinois v. B.C. and T.C.,* 680 N.E.2d 1355 (Illinois 1997), the Supreme Court of Illinois upheld this interpretation of the Illinois hate crimes statute, a law that was based on the ADL model. Because this controversy may arise in other states, some laws— for example, the Iowa hate crimes statute—specify that these affiliation cases are covered.

INDEX